JOY IN CHRIST'S PRESENCE

JOY IN CHRIST'S PRESENCE

CHARLES SPURGEON

Whitaker House

Unless otherwise indicated, all Scripture quotations are from the *King James Version* (KJV) of the Bible.

JOY IN CHRIST'S PRESENCE

ISBN: 0-88368-018-1
Printed in the United States of America
Copyright © 1997 by Whitaker House

Whitaker House
30 Hunt Valley Circle
New Kensington, PA 15068

Library of Congress Cataloging-in-Publication Data

Spurgeon, C. H. (Charles Haddon), 1834–1892.
    Joy in Christ's presence / by Charles Spurgeon.
       p.   cm.
    ISBN 0-88368-018-1 (pbk.)
      1. Christian life—Baptist authors.   I. Title.
BV4501.2.S71418   1997
248.4—dc21   97–40931

No part of this book may be reproduced or transmitted in any form or by any means, electronic or mechanical, including photocopying, recording, or by any information storage and retrieval system, without permission in writing from the publisher.

2 3 4 5 6 7 8 9 10 11 12 / 06 05 04 03 02 01 00 99 98

CONTENTS

Chapter 1

Mysterious Visits

Thou hast visited me in the night.
—Psalm 17:3

We ought to be amazed that the glorious God communicates with mankind, who are utterly sinful. *"What is man, that thou art mindful of him? and the son of man, that thou visitest him?"* (Ps. 8:4). A divine visit is a joy to be treasured whenever we are favored with it. David spoke of it with great solemnity. The psalmist was not content simply to mention it. Rather, he wrote it down in plain terms, so that it might be known throughout all generations: *"Thou hast visited me in the night."*

Beloved, if God has ever visited you, you also will marvel at it, will carry it in your memory, will speak of it to your friends, and will record it in your diary as one of the notable events of your life. Above all, you will speak of it to God Himself and say with adoring gratitude, *"Thou hast visited me in the night."* It should be a solemn part of worship to remember and make known the condescension of the Lord and to say, both in humble prayer and in joyful song, *"Thou hast visited me."*

7

To you, my dear readers, I will write of my own experience, not doubting at all that it is also yours. If our God has ever personally visited any of us by His Spirit, two results have accompanied the visit: it has been sharply searching, and it has been sweetly comforting.

THE RESULTS OF GOD'S VISITS

Our Hearts Are Searched

When the Lord first draws near to the heart, the trembling soul perceives clearly the searching character of His visit. Remember how Job answered the Lord: *"I have heard of thee by the hearing of the ear: but now mine eye seeth thee. Wherefore I abhor myself, and repent in dust and ashes"* (Job 42:5–6). We can read of God and hear of God and hardly be affected, but when we feel His presence, it is another matter.

I thought my house was good enough for kings, but when the King of Kings came to it, I saw that it was quite unfit for Him. I never would have known that sin is so *"exceeding sinful"* (Rom. 7:13) if I had not known that God is so perfectly holy. I never would have understood the depravity of my own nature if I had not known the holiness of God's nature.

When we see Jesus, we fall *"at his feet as dead"* (Rev. 1:17). Until then, we are full of vanity and pride. If letters of light traced by a mysterious hand upon the wall caused Belshazzar's knees to knock together and his legs to give way under him (Dan. 5:5–6), what awe overcomes our spirits when we see the Lord Himself! In the presence of so much light, our spots and wrinkles are revealed and we are utterly ashamed. We are like Daniel, who said, *"I was left alone, and saw this great vision, and there remained no strength in me: for my comeliness was turned in me into corruption"* (Dan. 10:8). It is when the Lord visits us that we see our nothingness and ask, "Lord, *'what is man?'"* (Ps. 8:4).

I remember well when God first visited me. It was a night of natural tendencies, of ignorance, of sin. His visit had the same effect on me that it had on Saul of Tarsus when the Lord spoke to him out of heaven. He brought me down off my high horse and caused me to fall to the ground. By the brightness of the light of His Spirit, He made me grope in conscious blindness; and in the brokenness of my heart I cried, *"Lord, what wilt thou have me to do?"* (Acts 9:6). I felt that I had been rebelling against the Lord, kicking *"against the pricks"* (v. 5) and doing evil as much as I could, and my soul was filled with anguish at the discovery of this.

The glance of the eye of Jesus was very searching, for it revealed my sin and caused me to go out and weep bitterly. As when the Lord visited Adam and called him to stand naked before Him, so was I stripped of all my righteousness before the face of the Most High. Yet the visit did not end there, for just as the Lord God clothed our first parents in coats of skins, He covered me with the righteousness of the Great Sacrifice and gave me songs in the night. It was night, but the visit was no dream. In fact, there and then I ceased to dream, and I began to deal with the reality of things.

I think you will remember that, when the Lord first visited you in the night, it was with you as it was with Peter when Jesus came to him. He had been toiling with his net the whole night, and nothing had come of it. But, when the Lord Jesus came into Peter's boat and told him to launch out into the deep and let down his net, he caught such a great multitude of fish that the boat began to sink. The boat went down, down, until the water threatened to engulf it along with Peter, the fish, and everything else. Then Peter fell down at Jesus' knees and cried, *"Depart from me; for I am a sinful man, O Lord"* (Luke 5:8). The presence of Jesus was too much for him; his sense of unworthiness made him sink like his boat and shrink away from the divine Lord.

I remember that sensation well. Indeed, I was half inclined to cry out, with the demoniac of Gadara, *"What have I to do with thee, Jesus, thou Son of the most high God?"* (Mark 5:7). My first discovery of Christ's injured love was overpowering, and its very hopefulness increased my anguish, for then I saw that I had slain the Lord who had come to save me. I saw that mine was the hand that had made the hammer fall, the hand that had driven the nails which fastened the Redeemer's hands and feet to the cruel tree.

This is the sight that breeds repentance: *"They shall look upon [Him] whom they have pierced, and they shall mourn for him"* (Zech. 12:10). When the Lord visits us, He humbles us, removes all hardness from our hearts, and leads us to the Savior's feet.

When the Lord first visited us in the night, it was similar to the way in which John was visited by the Lord on the isle of Patmos. John described it in the following words: *"And when I saw him, I fell at his feet as dead"* (Rev. 1:17). Yes, even when we begin to see that He has put away our sin and removed our guilt by His death, we feel as if we could never look up again, because we have been so cruel to our Best Friend. It is no wonder if we then say, "It is true that He has forgiven me, but I never can forgive myself. He makes me live, and I live in Him, but at the thought of His goodness I fall at His feet as dead. Boasting is dead, self is dead, and all desire for anything beyond my Lord is dead also." William Cowper poetically described this as

> That dear hour, that brought me to His foot,
> And cut up all my follies by the root.

The process of destroying follies is more hopefully performed at Jesus' feet than anywhere else. Oh, that the Lord would come again to us as He did at first, and like a consuming fire discover and destroy the dross that now alloys our gold! The word *visit* may remind those who travel of the person who searches their baggage. It is in a similar way that the Lord seeks out our secret things. But the word also reminds us of the visits of the physician, who not only finds out our sicknesses, but also aids and cures them. In this way did the Lord Jesus visit us at first.

We Find Sweet Comfort

Since those early days, I hope that you have had many visits from our Lord. Those first visits were, as I said, sharply searching, but the later ones have been sweetly comforting. Some of us have had them especially in the night, when we have been compelled to count the sleepless hours. "Heaven's gate opens when this world's is shut," I have heard it said. The night is still, visitors have gone away, work is done, care is forgotten, and then the Lord Himself draws near. Possibly there may be pain to be endured; your head may be aching, and your heart may be throbbing. But if Jesus comes to visit you, your bed of languishing becomes a throne of glory.

It is true that *"he giveth his beloved sleep"* (Ps. 127:2), yet at such times He gives them something better than sleep, namely, His own presence and the fullness of joy that comes with it (Ps. 16:11). At night, upon our beds, we have seen the unseen. Sometimes I have tried not to sleep while experiencing an excess of joy, when the company of Christ has been sweetly mine.

MANIFESTATIONS OF OUR LORD

"Thou hast visited me in the night." Believe me, there are such things as personal visits from Jesus to His people. He has not utterly left us. Though He may not be seen with our natural eyes near a bush or a running stream, nor on the mountain or by the sea, He still does come and go, observed only by our spirits, felt only by our hearts. He still stands behind our walls and shows Himself through the lattices (Song 2:9).

How can I describe these manifestations of the Lord? It is difficult for me to give you a good idea of them if you do not already know them for yourselves. If you had never tasted sweetness, no one could give you an idea of honey by describing it to you. Yet, if the honey is right in front of you, you can *"taste and see"* (Ps. 34:8). To a man born blind, sight must be a thing beyond his imagination; and to one who has never known the Lord, His visits are quite as much beyond what that person can conceive of.

More than Assurance of Salvation

For our Lord to visit us is something more than for us to have the assurance of our salvation, although that is very delightful, and none of us would be satisfied unless we possessed it. To know that Jesus loves me is one thing, but to be visited by Him in love is much more.

More than Picturing Christ

Nor is it simply a close contemplation of Christ, for we can picture Him as exceedingly fair and majestic and yet not have Him consciously near us. As delightful and instructive as it is to behold the likeness of Christ by meditation, the enjoyment of His actual presence is something more. I may wear my friend's picture around my neck, and yet I may not be able to say, *"Thou hast visited me."*

The Real Presence of Christ

The actual, though spiritual, coming of Christ is what we so much desire. The Catholic church says much about the *real* presence, meaning the physical presence, of the Lord Jesus. The priest who celebrates mass tells us that he believes in the real presence, but we reply, "No, you believe in knowing Christ according to the flesh, and in that sense the only real presence of Jesus is in heaven. We, on the other hand, firmly believe in the real presence of Christ that is spiritual, and yet certain."

By spiritual we do not mean unreal. In fact, the spiritual is what is most real to spiritual men. I believe in the true and real presence of Jesus with His people, for such a presence has been real to my spirit. Lord Jesus, You Yourself have visited me. As surely as Jesus came in the flesh to Bethlehem and Calvary, so surely does He come by His Spirit to His people in the hours of their communion with Him. We are as conscious of that presence as we are of our own existence.

THE EFFECTS OF CHRIST'S PRESENCE

When the Lord visits us in the night, what is the effect upon us? Our hearts meet His heart in a fellowship of love. Such communion first brings peace, then rest, and then joy in our souls. I am not writing of any emotional excitement that turns into fanatical rapture, but I mention a sober fact when I say that the Lord's great heart touches ours, and our hearts rise into empathy with Him.

First, we experience peace. All war is over, and a blessed peace is proclaimed; the peace of God keeps our hearts and minds through Christ Jesus (Phil. 4:7). At such a time there is a delightful sense of rest; we have no ambitions, no desires. A divine serenity and security envelop us. We have no thought of foes or fears, afflictions or doubts. There is a joyous laying aside of our own will. We are nothing, and we will nothing; Christ is everything, and His will is the pulse of our souls. We are perfectly content either to be ill or to be well, to be rich or to be poor, to be slandered or to be honored, so that we may simply abide in the love of Christ. Jesus fills the horizon of our beings.

At such a time, a flood of great joy will fill our minds. We will half wish that the morning may never break again, for fear that its light might banish the superior light of Christ's presence. We will wish that we could glide away with our Beloved to the place where He *"feedeth among the lilies"* (Song 2:16). We long to hear the voices of the white-robed armies (Rev. 7:9–10), so that we may follow their glorious Leader wherever He goes.

I am convinced that there is no great distance between heaven and earth, that the distance lies in our finite minds. When the Beloved visits us in the night, He turns our chambers into the vestibules of His palace halls. Earth rises to heaven when heaven comes down to earth.

14

GOD WILL VISIT YOU

Now, you may be saying to yourself, "I have not enjoyed such visits as these." Yet you may enjoy them. If the Father loves you even as He loves His Son, then you are on visiting terms with Him. Therefore, if He has not called on you, you will be wise to call on Him. Breathe a sigh to Him, and say,

> When wilt Thou come unto me, Lord?
> Oh come, my Lord most dear!
> Come near, come nearer, nearer still,
> I'm blest when Thou art near.

"As the hart panteth after the water brooks, so panteth my soul after thee, O God" (Ps. 42:1). If you long for Him, He much more longs for you. No sinner was ever half as eager for Christ as Christ is eager for the sinner; no saint was ever one-tenth as anxious to behold his Lord as his Lord is to behold him. If you are running to Christ, He is already near you. If you sigh for His presence, that sigh is the evidence that He is with you. He is with you even now; therefore, be glad.

Go forth, beloved, and talk with Jesus on the beach, for He often walked along the seashore. Commune with Him amid the olive groves, which were so dear to Him in many a night of wrestling prayer. Have your heart right with Him, and He will visit you often. Soon enough, you will walk every day with God, as Enoch did, and so turn weekdays into Sabbaths, meals into sacraments, homes into temples, and earth into heaven. May it be so with all believers! Amen.

Chapter 2

Under His Shadow

*He that dwelleth in the secret place
of the most High shall abide under the
shadow of the Almighty.
—Psalm 91:1*

I must confess that the outline for this chapter is borrowed. It is taken from one who will never complain about it, for to the great loss of the church she has left these lower choirs to sing above. Frances Ridley Havergal, the last and loveliest of our modern poets, has been caught up to add to the music of heaven. Her last poems were published with the title, "Under His Shadow," and the preface gives the reason for the name. In the preface she wrote,

> I should like the title to be, "Under His Shadow." I seem to see four pictures suggested by that: under the shadow of a rock, in a weary plain; under the shadow of a tree; closer still, under the shadow of His wing; nearest and closest, in the shadow of His hand. Surely that hand must be the pierced hand, which may oftentimes press us sorely, and yet evermore encircling, upholding, and shadowing.

17

In this chapter, I want to expound on the scriptural plan that Miss Havergal set down for us. Recall our text: *"He that dwelleth in the secret place of the most High shall abide under the shadow of the Almighty."* The shadow of God is not the occasional resort of the saint, but his constant abiding-place. Here we find not only our consolation, but also our habitation. We ought never to be out of the shadow of God.

It is to dwellers, not to visitors, that the Lord promises His protection. *"He that dwelleth in the secret place of the most High shall abide under the shadow of the Almighty,"* and that shadow will preserve him from the evil and *"terror by night"* (Ps. 91:5), from the arrows of war and of pestilence, from death and from destruction (vv. 5–6). Guarded by Omnipotence, the chosen of the Lord are always safe. For, as they dwell in the holy place, very near the mercy seat where the blood was sprinkled long ago, they are covered by the pillar of fire by night and the pillar of cloud by day, which continually hang over the sanctuary. Is it not written, *"In the time of trouble he shall hide me in his pavilion: in the secret of his tabernacle shall he hide me"* (Ps. 27:5)? What better security can we desire?

As the people of God, we are always under the protection of the Most High. Wherever we go, whatever we suffer, whatever our difficulties, temptations, trials, or perplexities may be, we are always *"under the shadow of the Almighty."* The tenderest care of a Guardian is extended over all who maintain their fellowship with God. Their heavenly Father Himself interposes between them and their adversaries. Yet, the experiences of the saints differ greatly from person to person. Though they are all under the shadow of God, they enjoy His protection in different ways—in fact, in the four different ways that

Frances Havergal mentioned in the preface to her collection of poems.

The Shadow of a Rock

I will begin with the first picture that Miss Havergal mentioned, namely, the rock sheltering the weary traveler. The prophet Isaiah spoke of *"the shadow of a great rock in a weary land"* (Isa. 32:2). Now, I take it that this is where we begin to know our Lord's shadow. At first, He was a refuge to us in time of trouble. The way was weary, and the heat was great; our lips were parched, and our souls were fainting; we looked for shelter, and we found none. We were in the wilderness of sin and condemnation, and who could bring us deliverance, or even hope?

A Hiding Place

Then we cried to the Lord in our trouble, and He led us to the Rock of Ages, which was carved for us long ago. We saw our Mediator coming between us and the fierce heat of justice, and we welcomed the blessed shield. The Lord Jesus was to us a covering for sin, and therefore a hiding place from wrath. The sense of divine displeasure, which had beaten upon our consciences, was removed by the removal of the sin itself. Our sin was laid on Jesus, who endured its penalty in our place.

A Complete Shelter

The shadow of a rock is remarkably cooling, and so was the Lord Jesus eminently comforting to us. The shade of a rock is denser, cooler, and more complete than any other shade. Beams of sunlight cannot reach through the rock and into its shade, nor can the heat penetrate as it will sometimes do through the foliage of a forest. Likewise, the peace that Jesus gives *"passeth all understanding"* (Phil. 4:7); there is no other like it. Jesus is a complete shelter, and blessed are they who are under His shadow. Let us take care that we abide there and never venture forth to answer for ourselves or to brave the accusations of Satan.

The Lord is the Rock of our refuge both from sin and from sorrow of every sort. No sun or heat can afflict us, because we are never out of Christ. The saints know where to fly, and they use their privilege.

> When troubles, like a burning sun,
>   Beat heavy on their head,
> To Christ their mighty Rock they run,
>   And find a pleasing shade.

Greatness, Not Gentleness

There is, however, something awesome about this great shadow. A very large rock is often so high that it is overwhelming, and we tremble in the presence of its greatness. The idea of littleness hiding behind massive greatness is set forth here, but there is no tender thought of fellowship or gentleness.

Looking only at this picture of the rock, we see the Lord Jesus as our shelter from the consuming heat of well-deserved punishment, but we know little more. Thus, it is very pleasant to remember that this is only one aspect of the fourfold picture. The deep, cool shade of the Rock, my blessed Lord, is inexpressibly dear to my soul as I, a sinner saved, stand in Him. Yet, there is more to it than this.

THE SHADOW OF A TREE

Our second picture is found in the Song of Solomon: *"As the apple tree among the trees of the wood, so is my beloved among the sons. I sat down under his shadow with great delight, and his fruit was sweet to my taste"* (Song 2:3). Here we have not so much refuge from trouble as special rest in times of joy.

The spouse was happily wandering through a wood, glancing at many trees and rejoicing in the music of the birds. One tree specially charmed her: the citron with its golden fruit won her admiration, and she sat down under its shadow with great delight. Such was her Beloved to her—the best among the good, the fairest of the fair, the joy of her joy, the light of her delight. Such is Jesus to the believing soul.

Rest for Our Souls

The sweet influences of Christ are intended to give us a happy rest, and we ought to avail ourselves of them. *"I sat down under his shadow"* (Song 2:3). Mary was blessed by taking advantage of the rest that Christ offered, while Martha nearly missed it in all her preparations for the meal. (See Luke 10:38–42.) This is the God-ordained way in which we are to walk, the way in which we *"find rest unto [our] souls"* (Matt 11:29).

Dear friends, is Christ to each one of us a place of sitting down? I do not mean a rest of idleness and self-content—God deliver us from that. But there is rest in a conscious understanding of Christ, a rest of contentment with Him as our all in all. I pray that God will cause us to know more of this!

Perpetual Solace

This shadow is also meant to yield perpetual solace, for the spouse in the Song of Solomon did not merely come under it, but she sat down as one who meant to stay. Continuance of repose and joy is purchased for us by our Lord's perfected work. Under the shadow she also found food. She had no need to leave it to find a single thing, for the tree yielded not only shade, but also fruit. She did not even need to rise from her rest, but as she sat still she feasted on the delicious fruit. You who know the Lord Jesus know also what this means.

The spouse never wished to go beyond her Lord. She knew no higher life than that of sitting under her Well Beloved's shadow. She passed the cedar, the oak, and every other tree, but the apple tree caught her attention, and there she sat down. *"There be many that say, Who will show us any good?"* (Ps. 4:6). But as for us, O Lord, our hearts are fixed (Ps. 57:7), resting on You. We will go no further, for You are our dwelling place (Ps. 90:1). We feel at home with You, and we sit down beneath Your shadow.

Some Christians cultivate reverence at the expense of childlike love. They kneel down, but they do not dare to sit down. Our divine Friend and Lover does not want it to be so; He does not wish to have us stand before Him in ceremony, but rather to come boldly unto Him (Heb. 4:16).

Delight in Christ's Presence

Let us use His sacred name as a common word, as a household word, and run to Him as to a dear familiar friend. Under His shadow we are to feel that we are at home. After that, He will make Himself at home to us by becoming food for our souls and by giving spiritual refreshment to us while we rest.

The spouse in the Song of Solomon did not say that she reached up to the tree to gather its fruit; but she sat down on the ground in intense delight, and the fruit came to her where she sat. It is wonderful how Christ will come down to souls who sit beneath His shadow. If we can only be at home with Christ, He will sweetly commune with us. Has He not said, *"Delight thyself also in the LORD; and he shall give thee the desires of thine heart"* (Ps. 37:4)?

With the tree, which is our second illustration of the Almighty's shadow, a sense of restful delight in Christ supersedes the sense of awe. Have you ever sat beneath the pleasing shade of that fruitful tree? Have you not only possessed security, but also experienced delight in Christ? Have you sung,

> I sat down under His shadow,
> Sat down with great delight;
> His fruit was sweet unto my taste,
> And pleasant to my sight?

This experience is as necessary as it is joyful— necessary for many reasons. *"The joy of the LORD is* [our] *strength"* (Neh. 8:10), and it is when we delight ourselves in the Lord that we have assurance of power in prayer. Here faith develops, and hope grows bright, while love sheds abroad all the fragrance of her sweet spices. Oh, dear reader, go to the apple tree, and find out who is the fairest among the fair. Make the Light of Heaven the delight of your heart, and then be filled with rest and revel in complete contentment.

The Shadow of His Wings

The third illustration of the shadow of the Almighty is that of the shadow of His wings. This is a precious word: *"Because thou hast been my help, therefore in the shadow of thy wings will I rejoice"* (Ps. 63:7). Does this Scripture not set forth our Lord as the One in whom we may trust in times of depression?

Earlier in this psalm, we read that David was banished from the means of grace to *"a dry and thirsty land, where no water* [was]*"* (v. 1). Moreover, he had fallen away from all conscious enjoyment of God. He said, *"Early will I seek thee: my soul thirsteth for thee"* (v. 1). Instead of singing about his present communion with God, he sang of memories.

Like David, we also have come into this condition and have been unable to find any immediate comfort. *"Thou hast been my help"* has been the highest note we could sing, and we have been glad even to reach that. At such times, the light of God's face has been withdrawn, but our faith has taught us to rejoice under the shadow of His wings. There has been no light, we have been completely in the shade, but it has been a warm shade. We have felt that God who has been near must be near us still, and therefore we have been quieted. Our God cannot change (Mal. 3:6); therefore, since He was our help, He must still be our help, even though He casts a shadow over us, for it must be the shadow of His own eternal wings.

The metaphor of wings is, of course, derived from the nestling of little birds under the shadow of their mother's wings, and the picture is unusually touching and comforting. The little bird is not yet able to take care of itself, so it cowers down under the mother, and there

24

it is happy and safe. Disturb a hen for a moment, and you will see all the little chicks huddling together and making a kind of song with their chirps. Then they push their heads into her feathers and seem happy beyond measure in their warm abode.

When we are very ill and extremely depressed, when we are concerned about our sick children, the troubles of a needy household, and the temptations of Satan, how comforting it is to run to our God! As the little chicks run to the hen, we can hide away near His heart, beneath His wings. Oh, tried ones, press closely to the loving heart of your Lord, hide yourselves entirely beneath His wings! Here, awe has disappeared, and rest itself is enhanced by the idea of loving trust. The little birds are safe in their mother's love, and we, too, are secure and happy beyond measure in the loving favor of the Lord.

THE SHADOW OF HIS HAND

The last illustration of the shadow is that of the hand, and this, it seems to me, points to power and position in service. Read Isaiah 49:2: *"And he hath made my mouth like a sharp sword; in the shadow of his hand hath he hid me, and made me a polished shaft; in his quiver hath he hid me."* This undoubtedly refers to the Savior, for notice what comes next:

[3] *And said unto me, Thou art my servant, O Israel, in whom I will be glorified.*
[4] *Then I said, I have laboured in vain, I have spent my strength for nought, and in vain: yet surely my judgment is with the LORD, and my work with my God.*
[5] *And now, saith the LORD that formed me from the womb to be his servant, to bring Jacob again to him, Though Israel be not gathered, yet shall I be glorious*

in the eyes of the LORD, and my God shall be my strength.
⁶*And he said, It is a light thing that thou shouldest be my servant to raise up the tribes of Jacob, and to restore the preserved of Israel: I will also give thee for a light to the Gentiles, that thou mayest be my salvation unto the end of the earth.*   *(Isa. 49:3–6)*

Our Lord Jesus Christ was hidden away in the hand of Jehovah, to be used by Him as a polished spear for the overthrow of His enemies and the victory of His people. Yet, inasmuch as it is true of Christ, it is also true of all of Christ's servants, *"because as he is, so are we in this world"* (1 John 4:17).

We may be sure that we are included with Christ in the hand of God, for the same expression is found in Isaiah 51:16, where, speaking of His people, He says, *"I have covered thee in the shadow of mine hand."* Is this not an excellent verse? Every one of you who will be a witness for Jesus will have a share in it. This is where those who are workers for Christ should long to be—*"in the shadow of* [His] *hand"*—in order to achieve His eternal purpose.

What are any of God's servants without their Lord? They are weapons that are out of the warrior's hand, that have no power to do anything. We ought to be like the arrows of the Lord, which He shoots at His enemies. His hand of power is so great, and we as His instruments are so little, that He hides us away in the hollow of His hand, unseen until He shoots us forth. As workers, we are to be hidden away in the hand of God; we are to be unseen until He uses us. To quote another verse, *"In his quiver hath he hid me"* (Isa. 49:2).

It is impossible for us not to be somewhat well-known if the Lord uses us, but we must not aim at being noticed. On the contrary, if we are used as much as the very chief of the apostles, we must truthfully add, *"though I be nothing"* (2 Cor. 12:11). Our desire should be that Christ should be glorified, and that self should be concealed.

But alas! There is always a way of showing self instead of Christ in what we do, and we are all too ready to fall into it. Suppose I went to visit a poor woman, but I did so with a great deal of arrogance. All that the woman would see would be that I had condescended to call upon her. But there is another way of doing the same thing so that the tried child of God will know that a beloved brother or a dear sister in Christ has shown sympathy for her and has come to minister to her heart.

There is a way of preaching in which a great theologian may clearly display his vast learning and talent, and there is another way of preaching in which a faithful servant of Jesus Christ, depending upon his Lord, may speak in his Master's name and leave a rich blessing behind. We ought to choose the way by which Christ may be glorified.

Within the hand of God lies the place of acceptance and safety, the place of power as well as of concealment. God only works with those who are in His hand, and the more we lie hidden there, the more surely He will use us before long. May the Lord do unto us according to His Word: *"I have put my words in thy mouth, and I have covered thee in the shadow of mine hand"* (Isa. 51:16).

In this case, we will feel all the former emotions combined: awe that the Lord would condescend to take us into His hand, rest and delight that He would stoop down so low to use us, trust that out of weakness we will now be made strong, and an absolute assurance that the purpose of our existence will be completed, for that which is urged onward by the Almighty's hand cannot miss its mark.

These thoughts cover only the surface of this subject, which deserves many more chapters than this one. Therefore, your best course will be to take these few hints and turn them into a long, personal experience of abiding under the shadow of the Almighty. May the Holy Spirit lead you into it and keep you there, for Jesus' sake!

Chapter 3

Under the Apple Tree

*I sat down under his shadow with
great delight, and his fruit was
sweet to my taste.*
—Song of Solomon 2:3

The spouse in the Song of Solomon knew her Beloved to be like a fruit-bearing tree, and so she sat under His shadow and fed upon His fruit. She knew Him, and she enjoyed His pleasures. It is a pity that we know so much about Christ and yet enjoy Him so little. Our experience ought to keep pace with our knowledge, and that experience should be composed of using what our Lord has given us in practical ways.

The way to learn a truth thoroughly is to learn it by experience, and the way to learn more is to use what you know. Jesus casts a shadow; let us sit under it. Jesus yields fruit; let us taste the sweetness of it. You know a doctrine beyond all doubt when you have proved it for yourself by personal test and trial. The bride in the Song of Solomon essentially said, "I am certain that my Beloved casts a shadow, for I have sat under it; and I am persuaded that He bears sweet fruit, for I have tasted it."

29

The best way to demonstrate the power of Christ to save is to trust in Him and be saved yourself. Out of all those who are sure of the truth of our holy faith, none are as certain as those who feel its divine power upon themselves. You may reason yourself into a belief of the Gospel, and you may, by further reasoning, keep a strict religious code; but a personal trial and an inward knowledge of the truth are incomparably the best evidences. If Jesus is like an apple tree among the trees of the wood, do not keep away from Him, but sit under His shadow and taste His fruit. He is a Savior; do not believe this fact and yet remain unsaved. As far as Christ is known to you, make use of Him in that measure. This is simple common sense!

Furthermore, we are at liberty to make every possible use of Christ. Both the shadow and the fruit may be enjoyed. Christ in His infinite condescension exists for needy souls. Oh, let me say it over again! It is a bold statement, but it is true: Christ Jesus our Lord exists for the benefit of His people. Just as a physician lives to heal, our Savior exists to save.

The Good Shepherd lives and has even died for His sheep. Our Lord has wrapped us around His heart, and we are intimately interwoven with all His positions of authority, with all His honors, with all His character traits, with all that He has done, and with all that He has yet to do. The sinners' Friend lives for sinners, and sinners may have Him and use what He has provided to the uttermost. He is as free to us as the air we breathe. What are fountains for, but that the thirsty may drink? What is the harbor for, but that storm-tossed ships may find refuge? What is Christ for, but that poor guilty ones like ourselves may come to Him and look and live, and afterward may have all our needs supplied out of His fullness?

Thus, the door is open to us, and we pray that the Holy Spirit may help us to enter in. I want you to notice in our text two things that you may enjoy to the full: first, the heart's rest in Christ, *"I sat down under his shadow with great delight"*; and, secondly, the heart's refreshment in Christ, *"His fruit was sweet to my taste."*

THE HEART'S REST IN CHRIST

A Valuable Rest

Let us notice the character of the person who uttered the sentence, *"I sat down under his shadow with great delight."* She was one who knew from experience what weary travel meant, and therefore she valued rest. Keep in mind that the person who has never labored knows nothing of the sweetness of repose. Also, the loafer who has eaten bread he never earned, who has never had a drop of honest sweat, does not deserve rest and does not know what it is. It is to the laborer that rest is sweet. So, when we come at last, toil-worn from many miles of weary plodding, to a shaded place where we may comfortably sit down, then we are filled with delight.

The spouse had been seeking her Beloved, and in looking for Him she had asked where she was likely to find Him. *"Tell me,"* she said, *"O thou whom my soul loveth, where thou feedest, where thou makest thy flock to rest at noon"* (Song 1:7). The answer was given to her, *"Go thy way forth by the footsteps of the flock"* (v. 8). She did go her way, but after a while she came to this resolution: "I will sit down under his shadow."

Many of you have been painfully wearied by attempting to find peace. Some of you tried ceremonies and trusted in them, and the priest came to your aid, but then he mocked your heart's distress. Others of you sought by various systems of thought to find an anchor; but, as you were tossed from wave to wave, you found no rest upon the seething sea of speculation.

Still others of you tried by your good works to gain rest for your consciences. You multiplied your prayers; you poured out floods of tears; you hoped, through giving to the poor and similar acts of charity, that some merit might come to you; and you hoped that your heart might find acceptance with God, and so have rest. You toiled and toiled, like the men who were in the vessel with Jonah when they rowed hard to bring their ship to land, but could not, *"for the sea wrought, and was tempestuous"* (Jonah 1:11). There was no escape for you that way, and so you were driven to another way, to rest in Jesus.

My heart looks back to the time when I was under a sense of sin, when I sought with all my soul to find peace but could not discover it, high or low, in any place beneath the sky. Yet, when I saw One hanging on a tree as the Substitute for sin, then my heart *"sat down under his shadow with great delight."* I began to reason in this way: Did Jesus suffer in my place? Then I will not suffer punishment. Did He bear my sin? Then I do not bear it. Did God accept His Son as my Substitute? Then He will never strike me down. Was Jesus acceptable to God as my Sacrifice? Then what contents the Lord should certainly content me. Consequently, I will go no farther, but I will sit down *"under his shadow"* and enjoy a delightful rest.

Shaded by His Sacrifice

She who said, *"I sat down under his shadow with great delight,"* could appreciate shade, for she had been sunburned. Her exclamation just before this was, *"Look not upon me, because I am black, because the sun hath looked upon me"* (Song 1:6). She knew what heat meant, what the burning sun meant; therefore, shade was pleasant to her.

You can know nothing about the deliciousness of shade until you travel in a thoroughly hot country; then you are delighted with it. Did you ever feel the heat of divine wrath? Did the great Sun—that Sun without *"variableness,* [or] *shadow of turning"* (James 1:17)— ever shoot His hottest rays upon you, the rays of His holiness and justice? Did you cower down beneath the scorching beams of that great Light and say, *"We are consumed by thine anger"* (Ps. 90:7)? If you have ever felt that, you have found it a very blessed thing to come under the shadow of Christ's atoning sacrifice.

A shadow, as you know, is cast by something that comes between us and the light and heat. Our Lord's most blessed body has come between us and the scorching sun of divine justice, so that we sit under the shadow of His mediation with great delight.

And now, if any other sun begins to scorch us, we run to our Lord. If we are oppressed by troubles at home or at work, or if we are tempted by Satan or led astray by inward corruption, we hurry to Jesus' shadow, to hide under Him and to sit down in the cool refreshment with great delight. Because our blessed Lord endured the heat of divine wrath, we may find an inward quiet. The sun cannot scorch us, for it scorched Him. Our troubles need not be troublesome to us, for He has taken our troubles, and we have left them in His hands. *"I sat down under his shadow."*

Take careful notice of these two things concerning the spouse. She knew what it was to be weary, and she

knew what it was to be sunburned. To the degree that
you know these two things, your esteem for Christ will
rise in proportion. You who have never wasted away under the wrath of God have never prized the Savior. Water is of small value in a land of streams and rivers, but if
you were making a day's march over burning sand, a cup
of cold water would be worth a king's ransom. In the
same way, Christ is precious to thirsty souls, but not to
anyone else.

Overshadowed by His Love

Now, when the spouse was sitting down, restful and
delighted, she was overshadowed. She said, *"I sat down
under his shadow."* I do not know a more delightful state
of mind than that of feeling overshadowed by our beloved Lord. I was black with sin, but His precious blood
overshadowed my sin and hid it forever. My natural condition was that of an enemy to God, but He who recon-
ciled me to God by His blood has overshadowed that also,
so that I now forget that I was once an enemy in my joy
of being a friend.

I am very weak, but He is strong, and His strength
overshadows my feebleness. I am very poor, but He has
all the riches of the universe, and His riches overshadow
my poverty. I am most unworthy, but He is so worthy
that if I use His name I will receive as much as if I were
worthy. Indeed, His worthiness overshadows my unworthiness.

It is very precious to put this truth another way and
say, "If there is anything good in me, it is not good when
I compare myself with Him, for His goodness quite
eclipses and overshadows it." Can I say I love Him? I do,
but I hardly dare to call it love, for His love overshadows

it. Do I think that I serve Him? I want to, but my poor service is not worth mentioning in comparison with what He has done for me. Have I thought that I had any degree of holiness? I must not deny what His Spirit works in me, but when I think of His immaculate life and all His divine perfections, where am I? What am I?

Have you not sometimes felt this? Have you not been so overshadowed by your Lord and hidden in Him that you became as nothing? I myself know what it is to feel that if I die in a poorhouse, it does not matter, as long as my Lord is glorified. Mortals may slander me (Luke 6:22), if they like, but what difference does it make, since His dear name will one day be written in stars across the sky? Let Him overshadow me; I delight that it should be so.

Spiritual Delight

The spouse told us that when she became quite overshadowed, then she felt great delight. When all you focus on is yourself, you never can have great delight, for you cannot bear to admit that something is greater than yourself. However, the humble believer finds his delight in being overshadowed by his Lord. In the shade of Jesus we have more delight than in any imaginary light of our own. The spouse had great delight. I trust that you, as a Christian, do have such great delight. If you don't, you ought to ask yourself whether you really are one of the people of God.

I like to see a cheerful countenance; yes, and I like to hear of overwhelming joy in the hearts of those who are God's saints! There are people who seem to think that religion and gloom are one and the same and can never be separated. They think that you must pull down the blinds on Sunday and darken the rooms. And if you have a garden, or a rose in bloom, you must try to forget that there are such beauties. They say, "Put your book under your arm, and crawl to your place of worship in as mournful a manner as if you were being marched to the whipping post. Are you not to serve God as miserably as you can?"

You may act this way if you like, but give me a religion that cheers my heart, fires my soul, and fills me with enthusiasm and delight, for that is likely to be the religion of heaven, and it agrees with the experience of the bride in the inspired Song of Solomon.

Although I trust that we know what delight means, I question whether we have enough of it to describe ourselves as sitting down in the enjoyment of it. Do you give yourselves enough time to sit at Jesus' feet? That is the place of delight—do you abide in it? Sit down under His shadow. "I have no time," someone may exclaim. Try to make a little. Steal it from your sleep if you cannot get it any other way. Grant leisure to your heart.

It would be a great pity if a man never spent five minutes with his wife, but was forced to be always hard at work. Why, that is slavery, is it not? Will we not then make time to commune with our beloved Lord? Surely, somehow or other, we can squeeze out a little time each day in which we have nothing else to do but to sit down under His shadow with great delight!

When I take my Bible, to feed on it for myself, I generally start to think about preaching on the passage of Scripture, and what I would say about it from the pulpit. I must get away from that and forget that there is a pulpit, so that I may sit personally at Jesus' feet. Oh, there is an intense delight in being overshadowed by Him! He is near you, and you know it. His dear presence is as certainly with you as if you could see Him, for His influence surrounds you.

I have often felt as if Jesus were leaning over me, as a friend might look over my shoulder. My heart grows calm when His cool shade comes over me. If you have been wearied by your family, or troubled over your church, or annoyed with yourself, you will come down from the place where you have seen your Lord and you will feel braced for the battle of life, ready for its troubles and its temptations, because you have seen the Lord. *"I sat down"* said the spouse, *"under his shadow with great delight."* How great that delight was she could not tell, but she sat down as one overpowered by it, needing to sit still under the load of bliss.

I do not like to talk much about the secret delights of Christians, because there are always some who do not understand my meaning. Even so, I will venture to say this much—that if worldlings could but even guess what are the secret joys of believers, they would give their eyes to share in them with us.

We have troubles, and we admit it; we expect to have them. But we also have joys in abundance. You know what this means, do you not? When you have been quite alone with the heavenly Bridegroom, you have wanted to tell the angels about the sweet love of Christ for you, a poor unworthy one. You have even wished to teach fresh music to the golden harps, for even the seraphim do not know the heights and depths of the grace of God as you know them.

The spouse had great delight, and we know that she did for this one reason: she did not forget it. This verse and the whole Song of Solomon are a remembrance of what she had enjoyed. She said, *"I sat down under his shadow."* It might have been a month ago, it might have been years ago, but she had not forgotten it. The joys of fellowship with God are written in marble. Memories of communion with Christ Jesus are engraved as in eternal brass.

"I knew a man," said the apostle, *"above fourteen years ago"* (2 Cor. 12:2). Ah, it was worth remembering all those years! He had not told of his delight, but he had kept it stored up. He said, *"I knew a man in Christ above fourteen years ago, (whether in the body, I cannot tell; or whether out of the body, I cannot tell: God knoweth)"* (v. 2), so great had his delights been.

When we look back, we forget birthdays, holidays, and nights that we have spent in the ways of the world, but we readily recall our times of fellowship with the Well Beloved. We have known our Mounts of Transfiguration, our times of fellowship with the glorified Christ, and like Peter we remember when we were *"with him in the holy mount"* (2 Pet. 1:18). Our heads have leaned against the Master's chest (John 13:23), and we can never forget the intense delight; nor will we fail to put on record for the good of others the joys with which we have been indulged.

How beautifully natural this is. There was a tree, and the spouse sat down under the shadow of it. There was nothing strained, nothing formal. In the same way, true piety should always be consistent with common sense, with that which seems most fitting, most becoming, most wise, and most natural. We have Christ, whom we may enjoy; let us not despise the privilege.

The Heart's Refreshment in Christ

Let us now look briefly at the heart's refreshment in Christ. *"His fruit was sweet to my taste."* I will not expound fully upon this, but I will give you some thoughts that you can work out for yourself later on.

The spouse did not feast upon the fruit of the tree until she was first under the shadow of it. There is no way to know the excellent things of Christ until you trust Him. Not a single sweet apple will fall to those who are outside the shadow. Come and trust Christ, and then you will enjoy all that there is in Christ. O unbelievers, what you miss! If you will only sit down under His shadow, you will have all things; but if you will not, no good thing of Christ's will be yours.

As soon as the spouse was under the shadow, the fruit was all hers. *"I sat down under his shadow,"* she said, and then, *"His fruit was sweet to my taste."* Do you believe in Jesus? Then Jesus Christ Himself is yours. And if you own the tree, you may very well eat the fruit. Since He Himself becomes yours altogether, then His redemption and the pardon that comes from it, His living power, His mighty intercession, the glories of His Second Advent, and all that belongs to Him are given to you for your personal and present use and enjoyment.

"All things are yours" (1 Cor. 3:21), since Christ is yours. Only be careful to imitate the spouse: when she found that the fruit was hers, she ate it. Copy her closely in this. A great fault in many believers is that they do not take the promises for themselves and feed on them. Do not err as they do. Under the shadow you have a right to eat the fruit. Do not deny yourself the sacred provision.

Labor Is Unnecessary

Now, as we read the text, it would appear that the spouse obtained this fruit without effort. Thomas Fuller, an English theologian and author, wrote, "He that would have the fruit must climb the tree." But the spouse did not climb, for she said, *"I sat down under his shadow."* I suppose the fruit dropped down to her. I know that it is so with us. We no longer *"spend* [our] *money for that which is not bread, and* [our] *labour for that which satisfieth not"* (Isa. 55:2), but we sit under our Lord's shadow, we eat that which is good, and our souls take delight in the sweetness. Come, Christian, enter into the calm rest of faith by sitting down beneath the cross, and you will be fed so that you are full.

The spouse rested while feasting; she sat and ate. So, believer, rest while you are feeding upon Christ! The spouse acknowledged that she sat and ate. Had she not told us in the preceding chapter that the King sat at His table (Song 1:12)? See how similar the church is to her Lord, how similar the believer is to his Savior! We sit down also, and we eat, even as the King does. His joy is in us (John 15:11), and His peace guards our hearts and minds (Phil. 4:7).

The Taste That Satisfies

Notice that, as the spouse fed upon this fruit, she had a relish for it. Not every tongue likes every fruit. Never dispute with other people about tastes of any sort, for agreement is not possible. The dessert that is the most delicious to one person is nauseating to another, and if there were a competition as to which fruit is preferable to all the rest, there would probably be almost as many opinions as there are fruits. But blessed is he who has a relish for Christ Jesus!

Dear reader, is He sweet to you? Then He is yours. There never was a heart that enjoyed the sweetness of

Christ unless Christ belonged to that heart. If you have been feeding on Him and He is sweet to you, go on feasting, for He who gave you the taste for His sweetness also gives you Himself to satisfy your appetite.

What are the fruits that come from Christ? Are they not peace with God, renewal of heart, joy in the Holy Spirit, love for the children of God? Are they not regeneration, justification, sanctification, adoption, and all the blessings of the covenant of grace? And are they not each and all sweet to our tastes? As we have fed upon them, have we not said, "Yes, these things are pleasant indeed. There is nothing else like them. Let us live upon them forevermore"?

Therefore, sit down, sit down and feed. It seems strange that we should have to persuade people to do this, but in the spiritual world things are very different from what they are in the natural. If you put a juicy steak and a knife and fork in front of most men, they do not need many arguments to persuade them to eat. Yet, they will not eat if they are full, whereas they will eat if they are hungry.

Likewise, if your soul is weary from longing for Christ the Savior, you will feed on Him; but if not, it is useless for me to write to you. However, you who are there, sitting under His shadow, may hear Him speak these words: "Eat, My friend, and drink abundantly." You cannot have too much of these good things. The more of Christ a person has, the better the Christian he is.

Christ, Our All in All

We know that the spouse feasted heartily upon this food from the tree of life, for in later days she wanted more. Read the fourth verse: *"He brought me to the banqueting house, and his banner over me was love"* (Song 2:4). Verse three describes, as it were, her first love for her Lord, her country love, her rustic love. She went to the wood, and she found Him there like an apple tree, and she enjoyed Him as one relishes a ripe apple in the country. But she grew in grace, she learned more about her Lord, and she found that her Best Beloved was a King.

I would not be at all surprised to find out that she there learned the doctrine of the Second Advent, for then she began to sing, *"He brought me to the banqueting house."* Essentially, she was saying, "He did not merely let me know Him out in the fields as the Christ in His humiliation, but He brought me into the royal palace. Moreover, since He is a King, He brought forth a banner with His own coat of arms, and He waved it over me while I was sitting at the table, and the motto of that banner was love."

She grew very full of this. It was such a grand thing to find a great Savior, a triumphant Savior, an exalted Savior! But it was too much for her, and her soul became sick with the excessive glory of what she had learned. Do you see what her heart craved? She longed for her first simple joys, those countrified delights. *"Comfort me with apples"* (Song 2:5), she said. Nothing but the old joys would revive her.

Did you ever feel like that? I have been satiated with delight in the love of Christ as a glorious exalted Savior when I have seen Him riding on His white horse and going forth to conquer (Rev. 6:2). I have been overwhelmed when I have beheld Him upon the throne, with all the brilliant assembly of angels and archangels adoring Him (Rev. 5:11–13). My thoughts have gone forward to the Day when He will descend with all the splendor of God and will make all kings and princes shrink into nothingness before the infinite majesty of His glory (Rev. 19:11–15).

Then I have felt as though, at the sight of Him, I must fall *"at his feet as dead"* (Rev. 1:17); and I have wanted somebody to come and tell me over again "the old, old story" of how He died so that I might be saved. His throne overpowers me; I want only to gather fruit from His cross. Bring me apples from "the tree" again. I am awestruck while in the palace; let me get away to the woods again.

Give me an apple plucked from the tree. Give me an apple such as this: *"Come unto me, all ye that labour and are heavy laden, and I will give you rest"* (Matt. 11:28). Or this: *"This man receiveth sinners"* (Luke 15:2). Give me a promise from the basket of the covenant. Give me the simplicity of Christ; let me be a child and feast on apples again, if Jesus is the apple tree. I would gladly meditate upon Christ dying on the cross in my place, Christ overshadowing me, Christ feeding me. This is the happiest state to live in. Lord, give us these apples forever!

You may recall the old story of Jack, a traveling salesman who used to sing,

> I'm a poor sinner, and nothing at all,
> But Jesus Christ is my all in all.

Those who knew him were astonished at his constant composure. They had a world of doubts and fears, and so they asked him why he never doubted.

"Well," said he, "I cannot doubt that I am a poor sinner, and nothing at all, for I know that and feel it every day. And why should I doubt that Jesus Christ is my all in all? For He says He is."

"Oh!" said one of his questioners, "I have my ups and downs."

"I don't," said Jack. "I can never go up, for I am a poor sinner and nothing at all, and I cannot go down, for Jesus Christ is my all in all."

When Jack wanted to join the church, the people said he must tell of his spiritual experience. He said, "All my experience is that I am a poor sinner, and nothing at all, and Jesus Christ is my all in all."

"Well," they said, "when you come before the church meeting, the minister may ask you questions."

"I can't help it," said Jack. "All I know I will tell you; and that is all I know. 'I'm a poor sinner, and nothing at all, but Jesus Christ is my all in all.'"

He was admitted into the church and continued to walk in holiness, but that was still the sum of his experience, and you could not get him beyond it.

"Why," said one brother, "I sometimes feel so full of grace, I feel so advanced in sanctification, that I begin to be very happy."

"I never do," said Jack. "I am a poor sinner and nothing at all."

"But then," said the other, "I go down again and think I am not saved, because I am not as sanctified as I used to be."

"But I never doubt my salvation," said Jack, "because Jesus Christ is my all in all, and He never changes."

That simple story is highly instructive, for it presents a simple man's faith in a simple salvation. This man is an example of a soul under the apple tree, resting in the shade and feasting on the fruit.

An Invitation

At this time I want you to think of Jesus, not as a Prince, but as an apple tree; and when you have done this, I pray that you will sit down under His shadow. It is not much to do. Any child can sit down in a shadow when he is hot. Next, I want you to feed on Jesus. Any simpleton can eat apples when they are ripe upon the tree. Come and take Christ, then.

You who have never come before, come now. Come and feel welcome. You who have come often, who have entered into the palace and who are sitting at the banqueting table, you lords and nobles of Christianity, come to the common wood and to the common apple tree where poor saints are shaded and fed. You had better come under the apple tree, like poor sinners such as I am, and be once more shaded with boughs and comforted with apples, or else you may faint beneath the palace glories. The best of saints are never better than when they again drink the milk of the Word and are comforted with the apples that were their first gospel feast.

May the Lord Himself bring forth to you His own sweet fruit! Amen.

Chapter 4

Over the Mountains

My beloved is mine, and I am his:
he feedeth among the lilies. Until
the day break, and the shadows flee away,
turn, my beloved, and be thou like a roe
or a young hart upon the mountains of Bether.
—Song of Solomon 2:16–17

It is possible that there are believers who are always at their best and are so happy that they never lose the light of their Father's countenance. But I am not sure that there are such people, for those believers with whom I have been most acquainted have had an experience of both highs and lows. And those of my acquaintances who have boasted of their constant perfection have not been the most reliable of individuals.

I always hope that there is an attainable spiritual region where there are no clouds to hide the Sun of our souls. However, I cannot be very positive about this, for I have not traversed that happy land. Every year of my life has had a winter as well as a summer, and every day has had its night. I have seen brilliant sunshine and heavy rains, and felt warm breezes and fierce winds.

Speaking for the majority of my brothers and sisters in Christ, I confess that, although the strength is in us, as it is in an oak tree, we do lose our leaves, and the sap within us does not flow with equal vigor during all seasons. We have our ups as well as our downs, our hills as well as our valleys. We are not always rejoicing; we are sometimes heavyhearted because of our various trials. Alas! We are grieved to confess that our fellowship with the Well Beloved is not always that of rapturous delight, but at times we have to seek Him and cry, *"Oh that I knew where I might find him!"* (Job 23:3).

This appears to me to have been, to a degree, the condition of the spouse when she cried, *"Until the day break, and the shadows flee away, turn, my beloved."* These words teach us several things.

COMMUNION MAY BE BROKEN

First of all, these words teach us that communion may be broken. The spouse had lost the company of her Bridegroom; conscious communion with Him was gone, though she loved her Lord and yearned for Him. In her loneliness she was sorrowful, but she had by no means ceased to love Him, for she called Him her Beloved and spoke as one who felt no doubt about that love.

Love for the Lord Jesus may be quite as true, and perhaps quite as strong, when we sit in darkness as when we walk in the light. The spouse had not lost her assurance of His love for her and of their mutual interest in one another, for she said, *"My beloved is mine, and I am his."* And yet she added, *"Turn, my beloved."* The condition of our blessings does not always coincide with the state of our joys. A person may be rich in faith and love, and yet have such a low self-image that he is greatly depressed.

It is clear from this sacred Canticle that the spouse loved and was loved, was confident in her Lord, and was fully assured of her possession of Him, and yet for the present there were mountains between her and Him. Yes, we may even be far advanced in the Christian life, and yet be exiled for a while from conscious fellowship with our Lord. There are nights for men as well as for infants, and the strong know as well as the sick and the feeble that the sun is hidden. Therefore, do not condemn yourself because a cloud is over you. Do not cast away your confidence. Rather, let faith be ignited in the gloom, and resolve in love to meet your Lord again, whatever the barriers may be that separate you from Him.

Sorrow and Darkness

When Jesus is absent from a true heir of heaven, sorrow will ensue. The healthier a person's condition, the sooner that absence will be perceived and the more deeply it will be mourned. This sorrow is described in the text as darkness, which is implied in the expression, *"Until the day break."* Until Christ appears, no day has dawned for us. We dwell in midnight darkness; the stars of the promises and the moon of experience yield no light of comfort until our Lord, like the sun, arises and ends the night. We must have Christ with us, or we are left to grope for the wall like blind men, and we wander in dismay.

Shadows in the Night

The spouse also spoke of shadows: *"Until the day break, and the shadows flee away."* Shadows are multiplied when the light of the sun departs, and these are apt to frighten those who are timid. We are not afraid of real enemies when Jesus is with us, but when we miss Him, we tremble at the smallest shadow. How sweet is that song, *"Yea, though I walk through the valley of the shadow of death, I will fear no evil: for thou art with me; thy rod and thy staff they comfort me"* (Ps. 23:4)! But we change our tune when night comes upon us and Jesus is not with us. Then, we fill the night with more terrors. Ghosts, demons, hobgoblins, and things that never existed, except in our imaginations, are apt to swarm about us, and we are in fear where no fear should exist.

Christ Turns His Back

The spouse's worst trouble was that the back of her Beloved was turned to her, and so she cried, *"Turn, my beloved."* When His face is toward her, she suns herself in His love; but if the light of His countenance is withdrawn, she is greatly troubled. Our Lord sometimes turns His face from His people, though He never turns His heart from His people. He may even close His eyes in sleep when the vessel is tossed by the tempest (Matt. 8:23–24), but His heart is awake all the while.

Even so, it is terrible enough that we have grieved Him in any degree; it pains us to think that we have wounded His tender heart. He is jealous, but never without cause. If He turns His back upon us for a while, He doubtless has a more than sufficient reason. He would not walk contrary to us if we did not walk contrary to Him (Lev. 26:23–24).

Ah, this is a sad situation! The presence of the Lord makes this life the preface to the celestial life; but His absence leaves us longing for Him, and no comfort remains in the land of our banishment. The Scriptures and the ordinances of the church, private devotion and public worship, are all like sundials—excellent when the sun shines, but of little use in the darkness. O Lord Jesus, nothing can compensate us for the loss of You! Draw near to Your beloved people yet again, for without You our night will never end.

Longings to Restore Communion

When communion with Christ is broken, there is a strong desire in all true hearts to win it back again. If a person loses the joy of communion with Christ, he will never be content until it is restored. Have you ever entertained Prince Immanuel? Has He gone elsewhere? Your heart will be a dreary place until He comes back again.

"Give me Christ, or else I will die," is the cry of every soul who has lost the dear companionship of Jesus. We do not part easily with such heavenly delights. With us it is not a matter of, "Maybe He will return, and we hope He will." Instead, "He must return, or we will become weak and die." We cannot live without Him, and this is a comforting sign, for the soul who cannot live without Him will not live without Him. He comes quickly when life and death depend on His coming. If you must have Christ, you will have Him. This is just how the matter stands: we must drink of this well or we will die of thirst; we must feed upon Jesus or our spirits will starve.

MOUNTAINS OF DIFFICULTY

I will now go further and say that when communion with Christ is broken, there are great difficulties on the path to its renewal. It is much easier to go downhill than to climb to the same height again. It is far easier to lose joy in God than to find the lost jewel.

The spouse spoke of *"mountains"* dividing her from her Beloved. By this, she meant that the difficulties were great. They were not little hills, but mountains, that blocked her way—mountains of remembered sin, alps of backsliding, ranges of forgetfulness, ingratitude, worldliness, coldness in prayer, frivolity, pride, unbelief. I cannot fully describe all the dark geography of this sad experience! Giant walls rose before her like the towering steeps of Lebanon. How could she approach her Beloved?

The difficulties that separated her from Him were many as well as great. The spouse did not speak of a single mountain, but of *"mountains."* Alps rose upon alps, wall after wall. She was distressed to think that in such a short time so much could come between her and Him of whom she had just sung, *"His left hand is under my head, and his right hand doth embrace me"* (Song 2:6). Alas! We multiply these *"mountains of Bether"* with a sad rapidity!

Our Lord is jealous, and we give Him far too much reason for hiding His face. A fault that seemed so small at the time we committed it is seen in the light of its own consequences, and then it grows and swells until it towers above and hides the face of the Beloved. Then our sun has gone down, and fear whispers, "Will His light ever return? Will it ever be daybreak? Will the shadows ever flee away?" It is easy to grieve away the heavenly sunlight, but ah, how hard to clear the skies and regain the unclouded brightness!

Uncertain Length of Separation

Perhaps the worst thought of all to the spouse was the fear that the dividing barrier might be permanent. It was high, but it might dissolve; the walls were many, but they might fall. But, alas, there were mountains, and these stand fast for ages! She felt like the psalmist when he cried, *"My sin is ever before me"* (Ps. 51:3). The pain of our Lord's absence becomes intolerable when we fear that we are hopelessly shut out from Him. A person can bear one night, hoping for the morning, but what if the day should never break?

If we have wandered away from Christ and feel that there are ranges of immovable mountains between Him and us, we feel sick at heart. We try to pray, but devotion dies on our lips. We attempt to approach the Lord at the communion table, but we feel more like Judas than John. At such times, we have felt that we would give our eyes to behold the Bridegroom's face once more and to know that He delights in us as He did in happier days. Still, there stand the awful mountains, black, threatening, impassable; and in the far-off land, the Life of our life is far away and grieved.

Insurmountable Difficulties

The spouse seemed to have come to the conclusion that the difficulties in her way were insurmountable by her own power. She did not even think of going over the mountains to her Beloved, but she cried, *"Until the day break, and the shadows flee away, turn, my beloved, and be thou like a roe or a young hart upon the mountains of Bether."* She did not try to climb the mountains; she knew she could not. If they had been lower, she might have attempted it, but their summits reached to heaven. If they had been less craggy or difficult, she might have tried to scale them; but these mountains were terrible, and no foot could stand upon their barren cliffs.

Oh, the mercy that comes with utter self-despair! I love to see a soul driven into a tight corner and forced to look to God alone. The end of the creature is the beginning of the Creator. Where the sinner ends, the Savior begins. If the mountains can be climbed, we will have to climb them; but if they are quite impassable, then the soul will cry out with the prophet,

> [1] *Oh that thou wouldest rend the heavens, that thou wouldest come down, that the mountains might flow down at thy presence.*
> [2] *As when the melting fire burneth, the fire causeth the waters to boil, to make thy name known to thine adversaries, that the nations may tremble at thy presence!*
> [3] *When thou didst terrible things which we looked not for, thou camest down, the mountains flowed down at thy presence.*　　　　　*(Isa. 64:1–3)*

Our souls are lame, they cannot go to Christ, and we turn our strong desires to Him and fix our hopes upon Him alone. Will He not remember us in love, and fly to us as He did to His servant of old when He *"rode upon a cherub, and did fly: yea, he did fly upon the wings of the wind"* (Ps. 18:10)?

A Prayer to the Lord

Now we come to the prayer of our text: *"Turn, my beloved, and be thou like a roe or a young hart upon the mountains of* [division]." Jesus can come to us when we cannot go to Him. The roe and the young hart live among the crags of the mountains and leap across the abyss with amazing agility. For swiftness and surefootedness, they are unrivaled.

The psalmist said, *"He maketh my feet like hinds' feet, and setteth me upon my high places"* (Ps. 18:33), alluding to the feet of animals that are created to stand securely on the side of a mountain. And so, the spouse in this golden Canticle sang, *"Behold, he cometh leaping upon the mountains, skipping upon the hills. My beloved is like a roe or a young hart"* (Song 2:8–9).

Christ Comes to Us

Here I would remind you that this prayer is one that we may justly offer, because it is Christ's way to come to us when our coming to Him is out of the question. "How?" you ask. I answer that He did this long ago, for we remember *"his great love wherewith he loved us, even when we were dead in sins"* (Eph. 2:4–5). When He came into the world in human form, was it not because man could never come to God until God had come to him? Our first parents offered no tears, prayers, or entreaties to God, but the offended Lord spontaneously gave the promise that the Seed of the woman would bruise the Serpent's head (Gen. 3:15). Our Lord's coming into the world was unbought, unsought, unthought of; He came altogether of His own free will, delighting to redeem.

Christ's incarnation was a foreshadowing of the way in which He comes to us by His Spirit. He saw that we were cast out, polluted, shameful, perishing; and as He passed by, His tender lips said, "Live!" In us the Scripture is fulfilled: *"I am found of them that sought me not"* (Isa. 65:1). We were too averse to holiness, too much in bondage to sin, ever to have returned to Him if He had not turned to us first.

What do you think of this? Did He not come to us when we were His enemies, and will He not visit us now that we are His friends? Did He not come to us when we were dead sinners, and will He not hear us now that we are weeping saints? If Christ came to the earth in this manner, and if He comes to each one of us in this fashion, we may well hope that now He will come to us in the same way, like the dew that refreshes the grass and *"tarrieth not for man, nor waiteth for the sons of men"* (Mic. 5:7).

Besides, He is coming again in person on the Last Day. Mountains of sin, error, idolatry, superstition, and oppression stand in the way of His kingdom, but He will surely come and overturn, and overturn, until He reigns over all. He will come in the last days, I say, though He will leap the hills to do it. Because of that, I am sure we may comfortably conclude that He will draw near to us who mourn His absence so bitterly. Therefore, we ought to go to Him and present the petition of our text: *"Turn, my beloved, and be thou like a roe or a young hart upon the mountains of* [division].*"*

He Knows Our Troubles

Our text gives us sweet assurance that our Lord is at home with difficulties that are, to us, quite insurmountable. Just as the roe or the young hart knows the mountain passes and the stepping places among the rugged rocks, just as it has no fear among the ravines and the precipices, so our Lord knows the heights and depths, the torrents and the caverns, of our sins and sorrows. He carried the entirety of our transgressions and so became aware of the tremendous load of our guilt. He is quite at home with the infirmities of our human nature; He knew temptation in the wilderness, heartbreak in the Garden, desertion on the cross.

He is quite at home with pain and weakness, for He *"Himself took our infirmities, and bare our sicknesses"* (Matt. 8:17). He is at home with despondency, for He was *"a man of sorrows, and acquainted with grief"* (Isa. 53:3). He is at home even with death, for He *"gave up the ghost"* (Mark 15:37) and passed through the sepulchre to resurrection.

O yawning gulfs and steep mountains of woe, our Beloved, like a deer, has traversed your glooms! O my Lord, You know everything that divides me from You. You also know that I am far too feeble to climb these dividing mountains so that I may approach You. Therefore, I pray, come over the mountains to meet my longing spirit! You know each cavernous abyss and every slippery slope, but none of these can hold You back. Hurry to me, Your servant, Your beloved, and let me again live by Your presence.

He Traverses the Mountains

It is easy, too, for Christ to come over the mountains for our relief. It is easy for the gazelle to cross the mountains; it was created for that purpose. Likewise, it is easy for Jesus, too, for He was ordained long ago to come to man in his worst condition, and to bring with Him the Father's love.

What is it that separates us from Christ? Is it a sense of sin? You have been pardoned once, and Jesus can renew most vividly a sense of full forgiveness. But you say, "Alas! I have sinned again, and fresh guilt weighs on my heart." He can remove it in an instant, for the fountain appointed for that purpose is open and is still full. It is easy for Redeeming Love to forgive the child's offenses, since He has already obtained pardon for the criminal's iniquities. If with His heart's blood He won our pardon from our Judge, He can easily enough bring us the forgiveness of our Father.

Oh, yes, it is easy enough for Christ to say again, *"Thy sins be forgiven thee"* (Matt. 9:2)! "But," you say, "I feel so unworthy, so unable to enjoy communion with Him." He who healed *"all manner of sickness and all manner of disease"* (Matt. 4:23) can heal your spiritual infirmities with a word. Remember the man whose ankle bones received strength, so that he ran and leaped. Remember the woman who was sick with a fever, who was healed at once and arose and ministered to her Lord. *"My grace is sufficient for thee: for my strength is made perfect in weakness"* (2 Cor. 12:9).

"But I have such afflictions, such troubles, such sorrows, that I am weighed down and cannot rise into joyful fellowship." Yes, but Jesus can make every burden light and cause each yoke to be easy (Matt. 11:30). Your trials can be made to aid your heavenward course instead of hindering it. I know all about those heavy burdens, and I perceive that you cannot lift them; but skillful engineers can adapt ropes and pulleys in such a way that heavy weights lift other weights. The Lord Jesus is the greatest of engineers, very skilled at the machinery of grace, and He can cause a weight of tribulation to lift from us a load of spiritual deadness, so that we can ascend by that which threatened to sink us down like a millstone.

What else hinders our way toward God? I am sure that, even if it were a sheer impossibility, the Lord Jesus could remove it, for *"the things which are impossible with men are possible with God"* (Luke 18:27). But someone objects, "I am so unworthy of Christ. I can understand eminent saints and beloved disciples being greatly indulged, but *'I am a worm, and no man'* (Ps. 22:6); I am utterly below such condescension." Do you really think so? Do you not know that the worthiness of Christ covers your unworthiness, and He *"is made unto* [you] *wisdom, and righteousness, and sanctification, and redemption"* (1 Cor. 1:30)?

In Christ, the Father does not consider you as low as you think you are. You are not worthy to be called His child, but He does call you so, and He considers you to be among His jewels. Listen, and you will hear Him say, *"Since thou wast precious in my sight, thou hast been honourable, and I have loved thee...I gave Egypt for thy ransom, Ethiopia and Seba for thee"* (Isa. 43:4, 3). Thus, there remains nothing that Jesus cannot leap over if He resolves to come to you and reestablish your broken fellowship.

He Is among Us

To conclude, our Lord can do all this immediately. As *"in the twinkling of an eye...the dead shall be raised incorruptible"* (1 Cor. 15:52), so in a moment our dead emotions can rise to fullness of delight. He can say to your mountain, *"Be thou removed, and be thou cast into the sea;* [and] *it shall be done"* (Matt. 21:21). Jesus is already among us. We do not have His physical presence, but we perceive His real spiritual presence. He has come. He speaks, saying, *"The winter is past, the rain is over and gone"* (v. 11).

And so it is; we feel that it is so. A heavenly springtime warms our frozen hearts. Like the spouse, we cry out with wonder, *"Or ever I was aware, my soul made me like the chariots of Amminadib"* (Song 6:12). Now in happy fellowship, we see the Beloved and hear His voice. Our hearts are ignited; our affections glow; we are happy, restful, brimming over with delight. The King has brought us into His banqueting house, and His banner over us is love (Song 2:4). It is a good place to be!

O Lord of our hearts, home is not home without You. Life is not life without You. Heaven itself would not be heaven if You were absent. Abide with us. The world is growing dark, the twilight of time is drawing near. Abide with us, for the evening is coming upon us. We are getting older, and we are nearing the night when the dew falls cold and chill. A great future is all around us; the splendors of the last age are descending; and while we wait in solemn, awestruck expectation, our hearts continually cry, *"Until the day break, and the shadows flee away, turn, my beloved, and be thou like a roe or a young hart upon the mountains of* [division].*"*

Chapter 5

Christ's Delight in His Church

Thou art all fair, my love;
there is no spot in thee.
—Song of Solomon 4:7

How marvelous are these words! *"Thou art all fair, my love; there is no spot in thee."* The glorious Bridegroom is charmed with His spouse, and He sings soft canticles of admiration. We do not wonder that the bride extols her Lord, for He well deserves it, and in Him there is room for praise without the possibility of flattery. But does He who is wiser than Solomon lower Himself to praise this sunburned Shulamite? Yes, for these are His own words, uttered by His own sweet lips.

O believer, do not doubt it, for there are more wonders to reveal! There are greater depths in heavenly things than you have yet dared to hope. The church not only is *"all fair"* in the eyes of her Beloved, but in one sense she always was so.

The Lord delighted in His children before they had either natural or spiritual beings, and from the beginning

He could say, *"My delights were with the sons of men"*
(Prov. 8:31). Having covenanted to be the Surety of the
elect (Heb. 7:22), and having determined to fulfill every
stipulation of that covenant, He, from all eternity, delighted to survey the purchase of His blood. Certainly,
He rejoiced to view His church, according to God's purpose and decree, as already delivered from sin by Him
and exalted to glory and happiness.

A Real Delight and Admiration

Now, with joy and gladness let us examine the subject of Christ's delight in His church. Christ has a high
esteem for His church. He does not blindly admire her
faults, nor does He conceal them from Himself. He is acquainted with her sin, in all its heinousness of guilt, and
He knows what sort of punishment is deserved. He does
not hesitate to reprove that sin. His own words are, *"As
many as I love, I rebuke and chasten"* (Rev. 3:19). He ab-
hors sin in her as much as in the ungodly world—even
more, for He sees in her an evil that is not to be found in
the transgressions of others, and this evil is the sin
against love and grace.

She is black in her own sight; how much more is she
so in the eyes of her omniscient Lord! Yet, there it
stands, written by the inspiration of the Holy Spirit and
flowing from the lips of the Bridegroom: *"Thou art all
fair, my love; there is no spot in thee."* How is this so? Is
it a mere exaggeration of love, an enthusiastic canticle,
which the sober hand of truth must strip of its glowing
fables? Oh, no!

The King is full of love, but He is not so overcome by
it that He forgets His reason. The words are true, and He
wants us to understand them as the honest expression of

His unbiased judgment after having patiently examined His spouse in every way. He would not have us diminish anything; rather, He would have us estimate the gold of His opinions by the brightness of His expressions. Therefore, so that there may be no mistake, He states it positively, *"Thou art all fair, my love,"* and confirms it by a negative, *"There is no spot in thee."*

Complete Admiration

When He speaks positively, how complete is His admiration! She is *"fair,"* but that is not a full description; He describes her as *"all fair."* He views her in Himself, washed in His sin-atoning blood and clothed in His meritorious righteousness, and He considers her to be full of loveliness and beauty. No wonder, since they are His own perfect excellencies that He admires.

The holiness, glory, and perfection of His church are His own garments, worn by His own well-beloved spouse, and she is *"bone of* [His] *bones, and flesh of* [His] *flesh"* (Gen. 2:23). She is not simply pure or well-proportioned; she is positively lovely and fair! She has actual merit! Her deformities of sin have been removed, but even more, she has through her Lord obtained a meritorious righteousness by which an actual beauty is conferred upon her. Believers are given a righteousness when they become *"accepted in the beloved"* (Eph. 1:6).

Fairest among Women

The church is not just barely lovely; she is superlatively so. Her Lord describes her as the *"fairest among women"* (Song 1:8). She has real worth and excellence that cannot be rivaled by all the nobility and royalty of the world. If Jesus could exchange His elect bride for all the queens and empresses of earth, or even for the angels in heaven, He would not, for He puts her first and foremost—*"fairest among women."*

This is certainly not an opinion that He is ashamed of, for He invites all men to hear it. He puts a *"behold"* before it, a special note of exclamation, inviting and arresting attention. *"Behold, thou art fair, my love; behold, thou art fair"* (Song 4:1). He publishes His opinion abroad even now, and one day from the throne of His glory He will avow the truth of it before the assembled universe. *"Come, ye blessed of my Father"* (Matt. 25:34) will be His solemn affirmation of the loveliness of His elect.

Repeated Praise

Let us note carefully His repeated praise for His spouse, the church.

> Lo, thou art fair! lo, thou art fair!
> Twice fair thou art, I say;
> My righteousness and graces are
> Thy double bright array.
>
> But since thy faith can hardly own
> My beauty put on thee;
> Behold! behold! Twice be it known
> Thou art all fair to Me!

He turns again to the spouse, looks into those doves' eyes of hers a second time, and listens to her lips that drip like a honeycomb (Song 4:11). It is not enough to say, *"Behold, thou art fair, my love."* No, He rings that golden bell again, and He sings again and again, *"Behold, thou art fair."*

After having surveyed her whole person with rapturous delight, He cannot be satisfied until He takes a second gaze and again recounts her beauties. With little difference between His first description and His last, he adds extraordinary expressions of love to prove His increased delight:

> [4] *Thou art beautiful, O my love, as Tirzah, comely as Jerusalem, terrible as an army with banners.*
> [5] *Turn away thine eyes from me, for they have overcome me: thy hair is as a flock of goats that appear from Gilead.*
> [6] *Thy teeth are as a flock of sheep which go up from the washing, whereof every one beareth twins, and there is not one barren among them.*
> [7] *As a piece of a pomegranate are thy temples within thy locks....*
> [9] *My dove, my undefiled is but one; she is the only one of her mother, she is the choice one of her that bare her.*   (Song 6:4–7, 9)

Universal Beauty

The beauty that Christ admires in His spouse is also universal; He is as much enchanted with her temples as with her breasts. All her forms of worship, all her pure devotion, all her earnest labor, all her constant sufferings, are precious to His heart. She is *"all fair."* Her ministry, her singing of psalms, her intercessory prayer, her benevolence and charity, her alertness to spiritual things—all are admirable to Him, when performed in the Spirit. Her faith, her love, her patience, her zeal, are alike in His esteem as *"rows of jewels"* and *"chains of gold"* (Song 1:10). He loves and admires everything about her.

In captivity, or in the land of Canaan, she is always fair. On the top of Lebanon, His heart is ravished with one of her eyes, and in the fields and villages He joyfully receives her love (Song 4:8–15). In the days of His gracious manifestations, He values her above gold and silver. But He has an equal appreciation for her when He withdraws Himself, for it was immediately after He had said, *"Until the day break, and the shadows flee away, I will get me to the mountain of myrrh, and to the hill of frankincense"* (v. 6), that He exclaimed, in the words of our text, *"Thou art all fair, my love."*

Whenever believers are very near the heart of the Lord Jesus, they are always like the apple of His eye (Deut. 32:10) and the jewel of His crown (Ezek. 16:12). Their names are still on His breastplate (Exod. 28:29), and their souls are still in His gracious remembrance. He never thinks lightly of His people, and certainly throughout His Word there is not one syllable that implies contempt of them. They are the choice treasure and the special portion of the Lord of Hosts. What king will undervalue his own inheritance? What loving husband will despise his own wife? Let others call the church what they may; Jesus does not waver in His love for her, and He does not differ in His opinion of her, for He still exclaims, *"How fair and how pleasant art thou, O love, for delights!"* (Song 7:6).

Let us remember that He who pronounces the church and each individual believer to be *"all fair"* is none other than the glorious Son of God, who is Very God of Very God. Hence, His declaration is final, since Infallibility has uttered it. There can be no mistake when the all-seeing Jehovah is the Judge. If He has pronounced the church to be incomparably fair, she is fair beyond a doubt. And though it is hard for our poor puny faith to receive, it is nevertheless as divine a truth as any of the indisputable doctrines of revelation.

A Confirmation of Praise

Having thus pronounced the church positively full of beauty, He now confirms His praise by a precious negative: *"There is no spot in thee."* It is as if the thought had occurred to the Bridegroom that the critical world would insinuate that He had only mentioned her beautiful parts and had purposely omitted those features that were deformed or defiled. So He sums up everything by declaring her universally and entirely fair, utterly devoid of stain.

A spot is often easily removed, and it may be the very least thing that can disfigure beauty, but the church is delivered in her Lord's sight even from this little blemish. If He had said, "There is no hideous scar, no horrible deformity, no filthy ulcer," we might even then have marvelled. But when He testifies that she is free from the slightest spot, all these things are included, and the depth of wonder is increased. If He had only promised to remove all spots, we would have had eternal reason for joy. But when He speaks of it as already done, who can restrain the most intense emotions of satisfaction and delight? O my soul, here is *"marrow and fatness"* (Ps. 63:5) for you; eat your fill, and be abundantly glad!

He Pardons and Loves Us Still

Christ Jesus has no quarrel with His spouse. She often wanders from Him and grieves His Holy Spirit. Nevertheless, He does not allow her faults to affect His love.

He sometimes chides, but it is always in the tenderest manner, with the kindest intentions—it is *"my love"* even then. He does not remember our follies; He does not cherish ill thoughts of us, but He pardons and loves after the offense as much as before it.

This is a good thing for us, for if Jesus were as mindful of injuries as we are, how could He commune with us? Many times a believer will put himself out of communion with the Lord because of some slight change in his circumstances, but our precious Husband knows our silly hearts too well to take any offense at our bad manners.

If He were as easily provoked as we are, who among us could hope for an accepting look or a kind greeting from Him? But He is *"ready to pardon...slow to anger"* (Neh. 9:17). He is like Noah's sons: He goes backward and throws a cloak over our nakedness (Gen. 9:23). Or we may compare Him to Apelles, who, when he painted Alexander, put his finger over the scar on his cheek, so that it might not be seen in the picture. *"He hath not beheld iniquity in Jacob, neither hath he seen perverseness in Israel"* (Num. 23:21), and so He is able to commune with the erring sons of men.

We Are "All Fair"

But the question remains: How can this be? Can this be explained even when sin remains in the hearts of the regenerate? Can our own daily distresses over sin ever allow anything like perfection to become a present attainment? The Lord Jesus says it, and therefore it must be true; but in what sense is it to be understood? How are we *"all fair,"* when we ourselves feel that we are *"black, because the sun hath looked upon* [us]" (Song

1:6)? We may easily grasp the answer when we consider the analogy of faith.

In the matter of justification, believers are complete and without sin. This is true with respect to the gift of Christ's righteousness that is imparted to believers. His beauty is put upon them, and it makes them very glorious and lovely, so that through Him they are beautiful beyond all others.

Dr. Gill excellently expressed the same idea when he wrote,

> Though all sin is seen by God, in *articulo providentiae*, in the matter of providence, wherein nothing escapes His all-seeing eye; yet in *articulo justificationis*, in the matter of justification, He sees no sin in His people, so as to reckon it to them, or condemn them for it; for they all stand *"holy and unblameable and unreproveable in his sight"* (Col. 1:22).

The blood of Jesus removes all stains, and His righteousness confers perfect beauty. Therefore, in the Beloved, the true believer is as much accepted and approved in the sight of God right now as he will be when he stands before the throne in heaven. The beauty of justification is at its fullness the moment a soul is received into the Lord Jesus by faith. This is righteousness so transcendent that no one can exaggerate its glorious merit. Since this righteousness is that of Jesus, the Son of God, it is therefore divine, and is, indeed, the holiness of God. Hence, Kent was not too daring when he sang,

> In thy Surety thou art free,
> His dear hands were pierced for thee;
> With His spotless vesture on,
> Holy as the Holy One.

Oh, the heights and depths of grace,
Shining with meridian blaze;
Here the sacred records show
Sinners black, but comely too!

But perhaps it is best to understand this as it relates to Christ's plans concerning His people. It is His purpose to present them without *"spot, or wrinkle, or any such thing"* (Eph. 5:27). They will be *"holy and unblameable and unreproveable"* (Col. 1:22) in the sight of the Omniscient God. In view of this, the church is seen as being virtually what she is soon to be in reality.

This is not a frivolous anticipation of the church's excellence, for we should always remember that the Representative, in whom she is accepted, is complete in all perfections and glories at this very moment. The Head of the body is already without sin, being none other than the Lord from heaven. It is in keeping with this truth that the whole body can be pronounced lovely and fair through the glory of the Head. The fact of the church's future perfection is so certain that it is spoken of as if it were already accomplished, and indeed it is so in the mind of Him to whom *"a thousand years* [are] *as one day"* (2 Pet. 3:8).

Let us magnify the name of our Jesus, who loves us so much that He will leap over the years of our pilgrimage that divide us from glory, so that He may give us even now the praise that seems to be appropriate only for the perfection of paradise.

ADMIRATION SWEETENED BY LOVE

The Lord addressed the spouse as *"my love."* The virgins called her *"fairest among women"* (Song 5:9); they saw and admired her, but it was reserved for her

Lord to love her. Who can fully describe the excellence of His love? Oh, how His heart goes out to His redeemed! As for the famed love of David and Jonathan, it is far exceeded in Christ. No tender husband was ever as fond as He is. No illustrations can completely reveal His heart's affection, for it surpasses all the love that man or woman has heard or thought of.

Expressions of Love

Our blessed Lord Himself, when He wanted to declare the greatness of His love, was compelled to compare one inconceivable thing with another in order to express His own thoughts. *"As the Father hath loved me, so have I loved you"* (John 15:9). All the eternity, fervency, immutability, and infinity that are to be found in the love of Jehovah the Father toward Jesus the Son, are copied exactly in the love of the Lord Jesus toward His chosen ones. Before the foundation of the world He loved His people; in all their wanderings He loved them, and to the end they will be loved by Him (John 13:1). He has given them the best proof of His affection. He gave Himself to die for their sins and opened the way for them to receive complete pardon as the result of His death.

His Willingness to Die

The willing manner of His death is further confirmation of His boundless love. How Christ delighted in the work of our redemption! *"Lo, I come: in the volume of the book it is written of me, I delight to do thy will, O my God"* (Ps. 40:7–8). When He came into the world to sacrifice His life for us, it was a freewill offering. *"I have a baptism to be baptized with"* (Luke 12:50). Christ was to be, as it were, baptized in His own blood.

How He thirsted for that time! *"How am I straitened till it be accomplished"* (v. 50). There was no hesitation, no desire to be rid of His responsibility. He went to His crucifixion without once stopping along the way to deliberate about whether He should complete His sacrifice. He paid for the tremendous mass of our fearful debt at once. He asked for neither a delay nor a reduction in suffering or punishment.

From the moment He said, *"Not my will, but thine, be done"* (Luke 22:42), His course was swift and unswerving, as if He had been hurrying to a crown rather than to a cross. The fullness of time (Gal. 4:4–5) was His only reminder; He was not forced to discharge the obligations of His church, but, even when He was full of sorrow, He joyously faced the law, answered its demands, and cried out, *"It is finished"* (John 19:30).

Oh, How He Loves!

How hard it is to talk of love in such a way as to convey what is really meant by it! How often have my eyes been full of tears when I have realized the thought that Jesus loves me! How my spirit has been melted within me at the assurance that He thinks of me and carries me in His heart! But I cannot kindle the same emotion in others, nor can I give, in writing, so much as a faint idea of the bliss that is contained in that exclamation, "Oh, how He loves!"

Dear reader, can you say of yourself, "He loved me"? (See Galatians 2:20.) Then look down into this sea of love, and try to guess its depth. Does it not stagger your faith that He loves you so? Or, if you have strong confidence, does it not enfold your spirit in a flame of admiration and adoring gratitude? Even the angels have never known such love as this! Jesus does not engrave their names upon His hands or call them His bride. No, this highest fellowship He reserves for worms such as ourselves, whose only response is tearful, hearty thanksgiving and love.

Chapter 6

The Beauty
of the Church

Behold, thou art fair, my love;
behold, thou art fair.
—Song of Solomon 4:1

As the bird returns often to its nest, and as the traveler hurries to his home, so does the mind continually pursue the object of its choice. We cannot look too often upon the face that we love; we desire always to have our precious things within sight. It is so even with our Lord Jesus. From all eternity, His *"delights were with the sons of men"* (Prov. 8:31). His thoughts rolled onward to the time when His elect would be born into the world; He viewed them in the mirror of His foreknowledge. The psalmist said, *"In thy book all my members were written, which in continuance were fashioned, when as yet there was none of them"* (Ps. 139:16).

When the world was set upon its pillars (1 Sam. 8:2), He was there, and He *"set the bounds of the people according to the number of the children of Israel"* (Deut. 32:8). Many times before His incarnation, He descended to this earth in the likeness of a man. The Son of Man visited His people on the plains of Mamre (Gen. 18:1–33), by the river of Jabbok (Gen. 32:22–30), beneath the walls of Jericho (Josh. 5:13–15), and in the fiery furnace of Babylon (Dan. 3:19–25). Because His soul delighted in them, He could not rest apart from them, for His heart longed for them. They were never absent from His heart, for He had written their names upon His hands (Isa. 49:16) and carried them on His heart (Exod. 28:29).

CHRIST REMEMBERS HIS PEOPLE

Just as the breastplate containing the names of the tribes of Israel was the most brilliant ornament worn by the high priest, so the names of Christ's elect were His most precious jewels, which He always hung nearest His heart. We may often forget to meditate upon the perfections of our Lord, but He never ceases to remember us. He does not care even half as much for any of His most glorious works as He does for His children.

Although His eye sees everything that has beauty and excellence in it, He never fixes His gaze anywhere with the admiration and delight that He spends upon His purchased ones. He charges His angels concerning them (Matt. 4:6), and He calls upon those holy beings to rejoice with Him over His lost sheep (Luke 15:4–7). He talks about them to Himself, and even on the tree of doom He did not cease to soliloquize concerning them. He saw the travail of His soul, and He was abundantly satisfied (Isa. 53:11).

Like a fond mother, Christ Jesus sees every dawning of excellence and every bud of goodness in us. He makes much of the beginnings of our graces, and He rejoices in them. As He is to be our endless song, so we are His perpetual prayer. When He is absent from us, He is still thinking of us, and in the black darkness He has a window through which He looks upon us. When the sun sets in one part of the earth, it rises in another place beyond our visible horizon. Likewise, Jesus, our Sun of Righteousness (Mal. 4:2), is pouring light upon His people in a different way, when to our understanding He seems to have set in darkness.

HE CANNOT FORGET HIS BRIDE

His eye is always upon the vineyard that is His church: *"I the LORD do keep it; I will water it every moment: lest any hurt it, I will keep it night and day"* (Isa. 27:3). He will not trust His angels to do it, for it is His delight to do everything with His own hands. Zion is in the center of His heart, and He cannot forget her, for every day His thoughts are set upon her. When the bride has neglected Him and hidden herself from His sight, He cannot be quiet until He looks upon her again. He calls her forth with the most wooing words:

14 *O my dove, that art in the clefts of the rock, in the secret places of the stairs, let me see thy countenance, let me hear thy voice; for sweet is thy voice, and thy countenance is comely.* (Song 2:14)

She thinks she is unfit to keep company with such a Prince, but He entices her from her hiding place. Inasmuch as she comes forth trembling, and bashfully hides her face with her veil, He asks her to uncover her face, to let her Husband gaze upon her. She is ashamed to do so, for she is black in her own eyes, and therefore He insists that she is beautiful to Him.

He is not content with merely looking, either. He must feed His ears as well as His eyes, and so He praises her speech and entreats her to let Him hear her voice. See how truly our Lord rejoices in us! Is this not unparalleled love? We have heard of princes who have been smitten by the beauty of a peasant's daughter, but what of that? Here is the Son of God doting upon a worm, looking with eyes of admiration upon a poor child of Adam and listening with joy to the lispings of poor flesh and blood. Should we not be exceedingly charmed by such matchless condescension? And should not our hearts as much delight in Him as He does in us? Oh, surprising truth! Christ Jesus rejoices over His poor, tempted, tried, and erring people.

CHRIST MAKES HIS LOVE KNOWN TO US

Sometimes the Lord Jesus tells His people His thoughts of love for them. Concerning this, Erskine once said,

> He does not think it enough behind her back to tell it, but in her very presence He says, *"Thou art fair, my love."* It is true, this is not His ordinary method; He is a wise lover, who knows when to keep back the intimation of love and when to let it out. But there are times when He will make no secret of it, times when He will put it beyond all dispute in the souls of His people.

The Spirit's Witness

The Holy Spirit is often pleased in a most gracious manner to confirm in our spirits the love Jesus has for us. He takes the things of Christ and reveals them to us. No voice is heard from the clouds, and no vision is seen in the night, but we have a testimony more sure than either of these. If an angel would fly from heaven and inform the believer personally of the Savior's love for him, the evidence would not be one bit more satisfactory than what is produced in the heart by the Holy Spirit. Ask those of the Lord's people who have lived nearest to the gates of heaven, and they will tell you that they have had seasons when the love of Christ toward them has been so clear and sure that they could no more doubt it than they could question their own existence.

His Presence Brings Confidence

Yes, beloved believer, you and I have had times of refreshment in the presence of the Lord, and then our faith has mounted to the uttermost heights of assurance. We have had confidence to lean our heads against the chest of our Lord, and we have had no more questions about our Master's affection than John had when he lay *"at his feet as dead"* (Rev. 1:17). The dark question, "Lord, am I the one who will betray You?" (Matt. 26:21–22), has been put far from us. He has kissed us with the kisses of His love (Song 1:2), and He has killed our doubts by the closeness of His embrace. His love has been sweeter than wine to our souls.

We felt that we could sing, *"His left hand* [is] *under my head, and his right hand* [does] *embrace me"* (Song 8:3). Then all earthly troubles were as light as the chaff on the threshing-floor, and the pleasures of the world were as tasteless as the white of an egg. We would have welcomed death as the messenger who would introduce us to our Lord, to whom we were eager to go. Christ's love had stirred us to desire more of Him, even His immediate and glorious presence.

Sometimes, when the Lord has assured me of His love, I have felt as if I could not contain more joy and delight. My eyes were filled with tears of gratitude. I fell upon my knees to bless Him, but I rose again in haste, feeling as if I had nothing more to ask for, but that I must stand up and praise Him. At such times I have lifted my hands to heaven, longing to fill my arms with Him, to talk with Him *"as a man speaketh unto his friend"* (Exod. 33:11), and to see Him in His own person. I have longed to tell Him how happy He has made His unworthy servant and to fall on my face and kiss His feet in unutterable thankfulness and love.

I have feasted upon one promise of my Beloved— *"Thou art mine"* (Isa. 43:1)—so much that I have wished, like Peter, to build tabernacles in that place and dwell there forever. But, alas, not all of us have yet learned how to preserve that blessed assurance. We stir up our Beloved and awake Him; then He leaves our uneasy hearts, and we grope after Him and make many weary journeys trying to find Him.

An Abiding Sense of His Love

If we were wiser and more careful, we might preserve the fragrance of Christ's words far longer, for they are not like the ordinary manna that soon rotted, but they are comparable to the little bit of it that was put in the golden pot and preserved for many generations. The sweet Lord Jesus has been known to write his love-thoughts on the hearts of His people in so clear and deep a manner, that they have for months, and even for years, enjoyed a continual sense of His affection. A few doubts have flitted across their minds like thin clouds before a summer's sun, but the warmth of their assurance has remained the same for many joyful days. Their paths have been smooth ones; they have fed in the green pastures beside the still waters, for His rod and staff have comforted them, and His right hand has led them.

I am inclined to think that there is more of this in the church than some people will admit to. We have a large number who dwell upon the hills and gaze on the light of the sun. They are the spiritual giants of the day, though the times do not allow them room to display their gigantic strength. In many humble beds, in many crowded workshops, in many modest homes there are people of the house of David, people after God's own heart, who are anointed with the holy oil.

It is, however, a mournful truth that whole ranks in the army of our Lord are composed of dwarfish "Littlefaiths," as in John Bunyan's *The Pilgrim's Progress*. People of fearful minds and despondent hearts are to be seen everywhere. Why is this? Is it the Master's fault or ours? Surely He cannot be blamed. It is then a matter of inquiry into our own souls: Can I not grow stronger? Must I be a mourner all my days? How can I get rid of my doubts? The answer must be: Yes, you can be comforted, but only the mouth of the Lord can do it, for anything less than this will be unsatisfactory.

Proof for the Asking

I do not doubt that there are ways in which those who are now weak and trembling may attain boldness in faith and confidence in hope. However, I do not see how this can happen unless the Lord Jesus Christ manifests His love to them and tells them of their union with Him.

This He will do, if we seek it of Him. The persistent pleader will not lack his reward.

Hurry to Him, O timid one, and tell Him that nothing will content you except a smile from His own face and a word from His own lips! Speak to Him and say, "Lord Jesus, I cannot rest unless I know that You love me! I desire to have proof of Your love by Your own hand and seal. I cannot live on guesses and surmises; nothing but certainty will satisfy my trembling heart. Lord, look upon me, if indeed You love me, and though I am less than the least of all believers, *'say unto my soul, I am thy salvation'* (Ps. 35:3)." When this prayer is heard, the castle of despair must totter; there is not one stone of it that can remain upon another if Christ whispers forth His love. As John Bunyan described it in *The Pilgrim's Progress,* even Mr. Despondency and his daughter, Muchafraid, will dance, and Mr. Ready-to-Halt will leap though he has been using crutches.

Oh, for more of these Bethel visits (Gen. 28:10–19), more frequent visitations from the God of Israel! Oh, how sweet to hear Him say to us, as He did to Abraham, *"Fear not, Abram: I am thy shield, and thy exceeding great reward"* (Gen. 15:1). To be addressed as Daniel was long ago, *"O man greatly beloved"* (Dan. 10:19), is worth a thousand ages of this world's joy. What more can a creature this side of heaven want to make him peaceful and happy than a plain avowal of love from his Lord's own lips? O Lord, let me always hear You. If You will only speak in mercy to my soul, I will ask no more while I dwell in the land of my pilgrimage!

Dear readers, let us work to obtain a confident assurance of the Lord's delight in us, for this will be one of the readiest ways to produce a similar feeling toward Him in our hearts. It enables Him to commune with us.

Christ is well pleased with us; let us approach Him with holy familiarity; let us pour out our thoughts to Him, for His delight in us will secure us an audience. The child may stay away from the father when he knows that he has aroused his father's displeasure, but why should we keep at a distance when Christ Jesus is smiling upon us? Rather, since His smiles attract us, let us enter into His courts and touch His golden scepter. O Holy Spirit, help us to live in happy fellowship with Him whose soul is knit to ours!

Chapter 7

Sweet Fellowship
with Christ

And of his fulness have all we received,
and grace for grace.
—John 1:16

The Lord Jesus has forever delighted Himself with the sons of men (Prov. 8:31), and He always stands prepared to reveal and communicate that delight to His people. But we are often incapable of returning His affection or enjoying His fellowship, having fallen into a state so base and degraded that we are dead to Him and have no regard for Him. Even so, something has been done for us and in us that allows us to converse with Jesus and to feel at one with Him.

Fellowship with Jesus is begun and maintained by giving and receiving, by communication and reception. I have selected one branch of this mutual communication as the subject for this chapter. Look closely at the text verse: *"And of his fulness have all we received, and grace for grace"* (John 1:16). As the life of grace is first begotten in us by the Lord Jesus, so is it constantly sustained by

Him. We are always drawing from this sacred fountain, always deriving sap from this divine root. Jesus communes with us as He bestows His mercies on us, and it is our privilege to have fellowship with Him as we receive them.

MISSED OPPORTUNITIES FOR FELLOWSHIP

There is this difference between Christ and ourselves: He never gives anything to us without manifesting fellowship, but we often receive from Him in such an insufficient manner that communion is not reciprocated. Therefore, we miss the heavenly opportunity of enjoying it. We frequently receive grace without realizing it. The sacred oil maintains our lamps, while we are ignorant of its hidden influence. We may also be the partakers of many mercies that, through our dullness, we do not perceive to be mercies at all. And at other times, blessings are recognized as such, but we are reluctant to trace them to their source in the covenant made with Christ Jesus.

We can easily believe that when the poor saints in Jerusalem received the contribution of the Christians in Macedonia and Achaia (Rom. 15:26), many of them acknowledged the fellowship that was demonstrated by the generous offering. But it is also likely that some of them merely looked upon the material nature of the gift and failed to see the spirit behind it.

Indeed, it is possible that, after a period of poverty, some of the receivers would be apt to give greater prominence to the fact that their need was removed than to the sentiment of fellowship with sympathizing Christians. They would rather rejoice over averted famine than the manifestation of fellowship. Undoubtedly, in many instances, the monetary contributions of the church fail to reveal our fellowship to our poor brothers and sisters, and they produce in them no feelings of communion with the givers.

Now, this sad fact is an illustration of the yet more distressing statement that I have made. Just as many of the partakers of the generosity of the church are not alive to the communion contained within the gifts, so the Lord's people are never sufficiently attentive to fellowship with Jesus in receiving His gifts. Instead, many of them forget that His gifts are a privilege, and all of them are not as aware of this as they could be. What is worse, believers often pervert the gifts of Jesus into food for their own sin and immorality!

We are not free from the fickleness of ancient Israel, and our Lord might very well address us in the language of the following passage:

> [8] *Now when I passed by thee, and looked upon thee, behold, thy time was the time of love; and I spread my skirt over thee, and covered thy nakedness: yea, I sware unto thee, and entered into a covenant with thee, saith the Lord GOD, and thou becamest mine.*
>
> [9] *Then washed I thee with water; yea, I thoroughly washed away thy blood from thee, and I anointed thee with oil.*
>
> [10] *I clothed thee also with broidered work, and shod thee with badgers' skin, and I girded thee about with fine linen, and I covered thee with silk.*
>
> [11] *I decked thee also with ornaments, and I put bracelets upon thy hands, and a chain on thy neck.*
>
> [12] *And I put a jewel on thy forehead, and earrings in thine ears, and a beautiful crown upon thine head.*
>
> [13] *Thus wast thou decked with gold and silver; and thy raiment was of fine linen, and silk, and broidered work; thou didst eat fine flour, and honey, and oil:*

*and thou wast exceeding beautiful, and thou didst
prosper into a kingdom.*
¹⁴ *And thy renown went forth among the heathen for
thy beauty: for it was perfect through my comeliness,
which I had put upon thee, saith the Lord GOD.*
¹⁵ *But thou didst trust in thine own beauty, and play-
edst the harlot because of thy renown. (Ezek. 16:8–15)*

Should not most of those who claim faith in God confess the truth of this accusation? Have not most of us
sadly departed from the purity of our love? We rejoice,
however, to observe a remnant of people who live near
the Lord and know the sweetness of fellowship. These
individuals receive the promise and the blessing, digest-
ing them so that they become good blood in their veins.
These people feed on their Lord so that they *"grow up
into him"* (Eph. 4:15). Let us imitate those elevated
minds and obtain their high delights.

MAINTAINING SWEET FELLOWSHIP WITH JESUS

There is no reason why the lowliest of us should not
be like David, who was a *"man after* [God's] *own heart"*
(1 Sam. 13:14). We may now be dwarfs, but growth is
possible. Let us therefore aim at a higher stature. With
the following advice and the Holy Spirit's help in carrying it through, we can attain the high position of those
who have and maintain sweet fellowship with the Lord.

Embrace Him at All Times

Make every time of need a time of embracing the
Lord. Do not leave the mercy seat until you have clasped
Him in your arms. In every time of need, He has prom-
ised to give grace to help you (Heb. 4:16). What holds you

back from obtaining the promised assistance, as well as sweet fellowship? Do not be like the beggar who is content with the charity of another, however grudgingly it may be given to him. Rather, since you are a relative of Christ, seek a smile and a kiss with every blessing He gives you.

Is He Himself not better than His mercies? What are they without Him? Cry aloud to Him, and let your petition reach His ears: "O my Lord, it is not enough for me to receive Your bounties, I must have You also. If You do not give me Yourself along with Your favors, they are of little use to me! Oh, smile on me when You bless me, for otherwise I still am not blessed! You put perfume into all the flowers of Your garden, and fragrance into Your spices; if You withdraw Yourself, they are no longer pleasant to me. Come, then, my Lord, and give me Your love with Your grace."

Take heed, Christian, that your own heart is right on key, so that when the fingers of mercy touch the strings they may resound with full notes of communion. How sad it is to receive a favor without rejoicing in it! Yet, such is often the believer's case. The Lord casts His lavish bounties at our doors, and we, like lowly peasants, scarcely look out to thank Him. Our ungrateful hearts and unthankful tongues mar our fellowship by causing us to miss a thousand opportunities for exercising it.

Draw upon His Supply of Grace

If you wish to enjoy communion with the Lord Jesus in receiving His grace, you must also endeavor to draw supplies from Him at all times. Make your needs public in the streets of your heart, and when the supply of grace is granted, let all the powers of your soul be present when you receive it. Let no mercy come into your house without giving thanks for it. Make note of all of your Master's benefits. Why should the Lord's bounties be hurried away in the dark or buried in forgetfulness? Always keep the gates of your soul open, and sit by the side of the road to watch the treasures of grace that God the Spirit hourly conveys into your heart from Jehovah-Jesus, your Lord.

Never let an hour pass without drawing upon the bank of heaven. If all your needs seem satisfied, look steadfastly until the next moment brings another need; and then do not delay, but with this proof of necessity, hurry again to your treasury. Your needs are so numerous that you will never lack a reason for petitioning the fullness of Jesus. However, if such an occasion should ever arise, enlarge your heart, and then love will fill the void.

Do not allow any supposed riches of your own to suspend your daily blessings from the Lord Jesus. You have constant need of Him. You need His intercession, His upholding, His sanctification; you need Him to carry out all your works in you and to preserve you until the Day when He appears again. There is not one moment of your life in which you can do without Christ. Therefore, be always at His door, and the needs that you complain of will be reminders to turn your heart toward your Savior.

Thirst makes a person pant for water, and pain reminds man of the physician. Let your needs likewise lead you to Jesus, and may the blessed Spirit reveal Him to you while He lovingly gives you the rich supplies of His love! Go, poor Christian, let your poverty be the rope that pulls you to your rich Brother. Rejoice that your weaknesses make room for grace to rest upon you, and be glad that you have constant needs that perpetually compel you to have fellowship with your Redeemer—who is worthy to be adored.

Study yourself. Seek out your needs, just as the housewife searches for rooms where she may store her things. Look upon your needs as rooms to be filled with more of the grace of Jesus, and allow no corner to be unoccupied. Long for more of Jesus. Let everything incite you to seek greater things.

Cry out to the Lord Jesus to fill the dry beds of your rivers until they overflow, and then empty the channels that have until now been filled with your own self-sufficiency. Ask Him to fill these also with His superabundant grace. If your heavy trials cause you to sink deeper in the flood of His consolations, be glad of them; and if your vessel sinks to its very bulwarks, be not afraid. I would be glad to feel the masthead of my soul twenty fathoms beneath the surface of such an ocean. As Rutherford said, "Oh, to be over the ears in this well! I would not have Christ's love entering into me, but I would enter into it and be swallowed up by that love."

Cultivate an insatiable hunger and an unquenchable thirst for this communion with Jesus through His communications. Let your heart cry forever, "Give, give," until it is filled in paradise.

> O'ercome with Jesu's condescending love,
> Brought into fellowship with Him and His,
> And feasting with Him in His house of wine,
> I'm sick of love,—and yet I pant for more
> Communications from my loving Lord.

This is the only covetousness that is allowable. But it is not merely beyond rebuke, it is also worthy of commendation. O believers, enlarge your desires and receive more of your Savior's measureless fullness! I charge you to hold continual fellowship with your Lord, since He invites and commands you to partake of His riches in this fashion.

Rejoice in Received Benefits

Let the satisfaction of your spirit overflow in streams of joy because of the benefits that you have received thus far from God's hand. When the believer rests all his confidence in Christ and delights in Him, it is an exercise of communion. Be glad in the Lord, and rejoice in His blessings!

Behold His favors, rich, free, and continual; will they be buried in unthankfulness? Will they be covered with a garment of ingratitude? No! I will praise Him. I must extol Him. Sweet Lord Jesus, let me kiss the dust of Your feet. Let me lose myself in thankfulness, for Your thoughts unto me are precious: *"how great is the sum of them"* (Ps. 139:17)! I embrace You in the arms of joy and gratitude, and in this I find my soul drawn to You!

This is a blessed method of fellowship. It is kissing the divine lips of grace with the sanctified lips of affection. Oh, for more rejoicing grace, more of the songs of the heart, more of the melody of the soul!

Recognize the Source of Mercies

Seek to recognize Him who is our Head as the only source of your mercies. Whenever chickens drink water, they lift up their heads to heaven after every drink, as if they are giving thanks. In the same manner, we ought to thank God for every blessing we receive, for He is the source of our blessings. If we have anything that is commendable and gracious, it comes from the Holy Spirit, and that Spirit is first bestowed on Jesus, and then through Him on us.

The oil was first poured on the head of Aaron, and from there it ran down upon his garments. Look upon your drops of grace, and remember that they come from the Head, Christ Jesus. All your rays come from this Sun of Righteousness, all your showers are poured out from this heaven, all your fountains spring from this great and immeasurable depth. Oh, for grace to see the hand of Jesus in every blessing, in every benefit! In this way communion will be constantly and firmly experienced.

May the Great Teacher, the Holy Spirit, perpetually direct us to Jesus by making the mercies of the covenant the signposts on the road that leads to Him. Happy is the believer who knows how to find the secret abode of his Beloved by tracking the footsteps of His loving providence. In this is wisdom. Dear Christian, work diligently to follow up every clue that your Master's grace reveals to you!

Maintain a Sense of Dependence

Sweet fellowship with Christ remains when you maintain a sense of your entire dependence upon His good will and pleasure for the continuance of your richest enjoyments. Never try to live on the old manna or to seek help in Egypt. All must come from Jesus, or you are forever ruined. Old anointings will not suffice; your head must have fresh oil poured upon it from the golden horn of the sanctuary, or its glory will cease.

Today you may be on the summit of the mount of God, but He who has put you there must keep you there, or you will sink far more quickly than you can imagine.

Your mountain only stands firm when He settles it in its place; if He hides His face, you will soon be troubled. If the Savior should see fit, there is not a window through which you now see the light of heaven that He could not darken in an instant. Joshua commanded the sun to stand still, but Jesus can shroud it in total darkness. He can withdraw the joy of your heart, the light of your eyes, and the strength of your life. In His hand your comforts lie, and at His will they can depart from you.

Oh, how rich is the grace that supplies us so continually and does not hold back because of our ingratitude! O Lord Jesus, we bow at Your feet, conscious of our utter inability to do anything without You. In every favor that we are privileged to receive, we adore Your blessed name and acknowledge Your inexhaustible love!

Admire God's Undiminished All-Sufficiency

When you have received much, admire the all-sufficiency that still remains undiminished. Thus, you will commune with Christ not only in what you obtain from Him, but also in the superabundance that remains treasured up in Him. Always remember that giving does not impoverish our Lord. When the clouds, those wandering cisterns of the skies, have poured floods upon the dry ground, an abundance remains in the storehouse of rain. Likewise, in Christ there is always an unbounded supply of grace, though the most liberal showers of grace have fallen ever since the foundation of the earth.

The sun is as bright as ever after all its shining, and the sea is quite as full after all moisture has been drawn from it to form clouds. In the same way, our Lord Jesus is always the same overflowing Fountain of fullness. All this is ours, and we may make it the subject of rejoicing fellowship. Come, believer, walk through the length and breadth of the land, for the land is yours as far as the eye can see, and much beyond that is also yours. It is all the gracious gift of your gracious Redeemer and Friend. Is there not ample reason for fellowship in this?

Be Assured by Every Mercy

Regard every spiritual mercy as an assurance of the Lord's communion with you. When a young man gives an engagement ring to the girl he wants to marry, she regards it as a symbol of his delight in her. Believer, do the same with the precious presents of your Lord. The common bounties of Providence are shared in by all men, for the good Householder provides water for His swine as well as for His children. Such things, therefore, are no proof of divine indifference.

But you have richer food to eat; *"the children's bread"* (Matt. 15:26) is your portion, and the heritage of the righteous is reserved for you. Therefore, consider every motion of grace in your heart as a pledge and sign of the moving of your Savior's heart toward you. His whole heart is in every mercy that He sends to you. He has impressed a kiss of love upon each gift, and He wants you to believe that every jewel of mercy is a symbol of His boundless love.

View your adoption, justification, and preservation as sweet enticements to fellowship with Christ. Let every note of the promise sound in your ears like the ringing of the bells of the house of your Lord, inviting you to come to the banquets of His love. Joseph sent donkeys laden with the good things of Egypt to his father, and good old Jacob undoubtedly regarded them as pledges of the love of his son's heart. Be sure not to think less of the kindnesses of Jesus.

Know the Value of His Blessings

Study to know the value of His blessings. They are not ordinary things, like costume jewelry or imitation gemstones. Instead, every one of them is so costly that, if all heaven had been drained of treasure, apart from the precious offering of the Redeemer, not even the least of His benefits could have been purchased. When you see your pardon, consider how great a blessing is contained in it! Hell would have been your eternal portion if Christ had not plucked you from the fire!

When you are enabled to see yourself as clothed in the imputed righteousness of Jesus, admire the profusion of precious things of which your robe is made. Think how many times the Man of Sorrows wearied Himself at that loom of obedience on which He wove that matchless garment. And think, if you can, how many worlds of merit were put into the fabric every time a new thread was woven into it!

Remember that all the angels in heaven could not have provided Him with a single thread that would have been rich enough to weave into the texture of His perfect righteousness. Consider the cost of your maintenance for an hour; remember that your needs are so large that all the storehouses of grace that believers could fill could not feed you for a moment.

What an expensive dependent you are! King Solomon made marvelous provision for his household (1 Kings 4:22), but all his meat and fine flour would be like a drop in the bucket compared with your daily needs. Rivers of oil and ten thousand cattle (see Micah 6:7) would not provide enough to supply the necessities of your hungering soul. Your smallest spiritual need demands infinity to satisfy it. The sum total of your perpetually repeated demands upon the Lord must be amazing!

Arise, then, and bless the Lord for the invaluable riches with which He has endowed you. See what a dowry your Bridegroom has brought to His poor, penniless spouse. He knows the value of the blessings that He brings to you, for He has paid for them out of His heart's richest blood. Do not be so ungenerous as to overlook them as if they were worth only a little. Poor men know more of the value of money than those who have always reveled in an abundance of wealth. Should not your former poverty teach you the preciousness of the grace that Jesus gives? Remember, there was a time when you would have given a thousand worlds, if they had been yours, in order to procure the very least of His abundant mercies.

Remember Your Salvation

Remember how impossible it would have been for you to receive a single spiritual blessing if you had not been in Jesus. The love of God cannot be poured out into anyone's heart unless he is clearly united with God's Son. No exception has ever been made to the universal curse on those of the first Adam's seed who have no interest in the Second Adam. Christ is the only Zoar in which God's Lots can find a shelter from the destruction of Sodom (Gen. 19:15–25). Apart from Him, the blast of the fiery furnace of God's wrath consumes every green herb; it is only in Him that the soul can live.

When a field is on fire, people see sheets of flame shooting up into the sky, and in haste they flee before the devouring element. Yet they have one hope: in the distance there is a lake of water. They reach it, they plunge into it, and they are safe. Although the skies are molten with the heat, the sun darkened with the smoke, and the field utterly consumed in the fire, they know that they are secure while the cooling flood embraces them.

Likewise, Christ Jesus is the only escape for a sinner pursued by the fiery wrath of God, and every believer ought to remember this. Our own works could never shelter us, for they have proved to be only refuges of lies. Even if they had been a thousand times more and better, they would have been only as the spider's web, too frail to hang eternal interests upon. There is only one name, one sacrifice, one blood, by which we may escape. All other attempts at salvation are a grievous failure.

How, then, with your innumerable sins, have you escaped the damnation of hell, much less become the recipient of bounties so rich and large? Blessed Window of Heaven, sweet Lord Jesus, let Your church forever adore You as the only channel by which mercies can flow to her. My soul, give Him continual praise, for without Him you would have been poorer than a beggar. Be mindful, O heir of heaven, that you could not have had one ray of hope or one word of comfort if you had not been in union with Christ Jesus! The crumbs that fall from your table are more than grace itself would have given you if you had not been loved and approved in Jesus.

Everything that you have, you have in Him; you have been chosen in Him, redeemed in Him, justified in Him, accepted in Him. You are risen in Him, but without Him you would have died the second death. In Him you are raised up to the heavenly places, but out of Him you would have been damned eternally.

Bless Him, then. Ask the angels to bless Him. Rouse all ages to a harmony of praise for His condescending love in taking poor, guilty nothings into oneness with Himself—who is completely worthy of adoration. This is a blessed means of promoting communion. The sacred Comforter is pleased to take of the things of Christ and reveal them to us as ours, but they are only ours as we are in Him. Holy Jesus, let us never forget that we are members of Your spiritual body and that we are blessed and preserved for this reason.

Think of What Christ Endured

Meditate upon the gracious acts that procured such blessings for you. Consider the labors that your Lord endured for you and the sufferings by which He purchased the mercies that He bestows. What human tongue can describe the unutterable misery of His heart or tell so much as one of the agonies that crowded upon His soul? How much less can we comprehend the vast total of Christ's sufferings! But all His sorrows were necessary for your benefit, and without them not one of your innumerable mercies could have been bestowed. Keep in mind that

> There's ne'er a gift His hand bestows,
> But cost His heart a groan.

Look upon the frozen ground of Gethsemane, and behold the bloody sweat that stained the soil! Turn to the hall of Gabbatha, and see the victim of justice pursued by His insistent foes! Enter the guardroom of the Praetorians, and view the spitting, and the plucking of His hair! Then conclude your review upon Golgotha, the mount of doom, where death consummated His tortures. If, by divine assistance, you are enabled to enter, in some humble measure, into the depths of your Lord's sufferings, you will be better prepared to hold fellowship with Him the next time you receive His priceless gifts. In proportion to your sense of their costliness will be your capacity for enjoying the love that is centered in them.

Never Forget That Christ Is Yours

Above all, never forget that Christ is yours. Amid the profusion of His gifts, never forget that the chief gift is Himself; and do not forget that, after all, His gifts are but Himself. He clothes you, but it is with Himself, with His own spotless righteousness and character. He washes you, but His innermost self, His own heart's blood, is the stream with which the fountain overflows. He feeds you with the bread of heaven, but do not forget that the bread is Himself, His own body that He gives as the food of souls.

Never be satisfied with something less than a whole Christ. A wife will not be put off with jewels and attire—these will be nothing to her unless she can call her husband's heart and person her own. It was the passover lamb upon which the ancient Israelites feasted on that night that was never to be forgotten. In the same way, feast on Jesus, and on nothing less than Jesus, for anything less than Him will be food too light for your soul's satisfaction. Oh, be careful to eat His flesh and drink His blood, and so receive Him into yourself in a real and spiritual manner, for nothing but this will be an evidence of eternal life in your soul!

Is there more that I can add to these instructions for maintaining fellowship with our Lord? One great exhortation remains, which must not be omitted: seek the abundant assistance of the Holy Spirit to enable you to put these things into practice, for without His aid, all that I have written here will be like tormenting the lame with rules for walking, or the dying with regulations for the preservation of health. O Divine Spirit, while we enjoy the grace of Jesus, lead us into the secret abode of our Lord, so that we may eat with Him, and He with us. Grant unto us hourly grace, so that we may continue in the company of our Lord from the rising to the setting of the sun! Amen.

Chapter 8

Redeemed Souls Freed from Fear

Fear not: for I have redeemed thee.
—Isaiah 43:1

I have been lamenting my unfitness for my work, especially for the warfare to which I am called. A sense of
heaviness recently came over me, but relief came very
quickly, for which I thank the Lord. Indeed, I was greatly
burdened, but the Lord comforted me with the words of
Isaiah 43:1: *"But now thus saith the LORD that created
thee, O Jacob, and he that formed thee, O Israel, Fear
not."* I said to myself, "I am what God created me to be,
and I am what He formed me to be. Therefore, I must,
after all, be the right man for the place in which He has
put me." We are in no position to blame our Creator or
to suspect that He has missed His mark in forming an
instrument for His work. When we understand this, new
comfort will come to us.

Not only do the operations of grace in the spiritual
world give us consolation, but we are also comforted by
what the Lord has done in creation. We are told to cease

being afraid, and we do so because we perceive that it is the Lord who made us, and not we ourselves. He will be the One to justify His own creative skills by accomplishing through us the purposes of His love.

The next sentence of Isaiah 43 is usually very comforting to my soul. The verse goes on to say, *"Fear not: for I have redeemed thee."* Think for a few minutes of the wonderful depth of consolation that lies in this fact. We have been redeemed by the Lord Himself, and this is a major reason why we should never again be subject to fear. Oh, that the logic of this fact could be turned into practice, so that from now on we would rejoice, or at least feel the peace of God!

In Times of Trouble

These words of our text verse may be spoken, first of all, concerning those frequent occasions in which the Lord has redeemed His people out of trouble. Many a time might our Lord say to each one of us, *"I have redeemed thee."* Out of six, yes, even six thousand trials He has rescued us by the right hand of His power. He has released us from our afflictions (Ps. 34:19), and He *"broughtest us out into a wealthy place"* (Ps. 66:12).

In the remembrance of all these redemptions the Lord seems to say to us, "What I have done before, I will do again. I have redeemed you, and I will still redeem you. I have brought you from under the hand of the oppressor; I have delivered you from the tongue of the slanderer; I have borne you up under the load of poverty and sustained you under the pains of sickness; and I am able still to do the same. Why, then, do you fear? Why should you be afraid, since already I have again and again redeemed you? Take heart, and be confident, for even to old age and to death itself I will continue to be your strong Redeemer."

Looking again at our text verse, I suppose it could refer to the great redemption out of Egypt. This statement was addressed to the people of God under captivity in Babylon, and we know that the Lord referred to the Egyptian redemption, for He said in the third verse, *"I gave Egypt for thy ransom."* Egypt was a great country and a rich country, for we read of *"the treasures in Egypt"* (Heb. 11:26), but God would give all the nations of the earth for His Israel. This was a wonderful comfort to the people of God; they constantly referred to Egypt and the Red Sea, and they made their national anthem out of it.

In all Israel's times of disaster and calamity and trial, they joyfully remembered that the Lord had redeemed them when they were a company of slaves, helpless and hopeless, under a tyrant who cast their firstborn children into the Nile, a tyrant whose power was so tremendous that all the armies of the world could not have wrested their deliverance from his iron hand. The very nod of Pharaoh seemed to the inhabitants of Egypt to be omnipotent; he was a builder of pyramids, a master of all the sciences of peace and the arts of war. What could the Israelites have done against him?

Jehovah came to their relief in their dire extremity. His plagues followed each other in quick succession. The awe-inspiring volleys of the Lord's artillery confounded His foes. At last He killed all the firstborn of Egypt, the most valuable part of all their strength. Then Egypt was glad that Israel departed, and the Lord brought forth His people with silver and gold. All the army of Egypt was overthrown and destroyed in the Red Sea, and the timbrels of the daughters of Israel sounded joyously upon its shores.

This redemption out of Egypt was so remarkable that it is remembered even in heaven. The Old Testament song is woven into that of the new covenant, for the redeemed *"sing the song of Moses the servant of God, and the song of the Lamb"* (Rev. 15:3). The first redemption was such a wonderful type and prophecy of the other that it will be held in memory forever and ever. Every Israelite must have had confidence in God after what He had done for the people in redeeming them out of Egypt. Every one of the seed of Jacob had an excellent reason to *"fear not."*

Nevertheless, I interpret these words as a reference to the redemption that has been bought for us by Him who loved us and washed us from our sins by His own blood. Let us think of it in this way, too.

IN TIMES OF PERPLEXITY

The remembrance of this transcendent redemption ought to comfort us in all times of perplexity. When we cannot see our way or cannot determine what to do, we do not need to be troubled at all concerning it, for the Lord Jehovah can see a way out of every complication.

There was never a problem so difficult to solve as that which is answered in redemption. The tremendous difficulty was in this: How can God be just and yet be the Savior of sinners? How can He fulfill His declarations against evil and yet forgive sin? If that problem had been left to angels and men, they could never have worked it out throughout eternity. But God has solved it by freely delivering up His own Son.

In the glorious sacrifice of Jesus we see the justice of God magnified. He placed the whole weight of sin on the

106

blessed Lord, who had become one with His chosen people. Jesus identified Himself with His people, and therefore their sin was laid upon Him, and the sword of the Lord awoke against Him. He was not taken arbitrarily to be a victim, but He was a voluntary Sufferer. His relationship amounted to covenant oneness with His people, and *"it behoved Christ to suffer"* (Luke 24:46).

There is a wisdom in this that overcomes all minor perplexities. Take this into account, then, you poor soul in suspense! The Lord says, *"'I have redeemed thee.'* I have already brought you out of the labyrinth in which you were lost because of sin, and therefore I will take you out of the meshes of the net of temptation and will lead you through the maze of trial. *'I will bring the blind by a way that they* [know] *not; I will lead them in paths that they have not known'* (Isa. 42:16). *'I will bring again from Bashan, I will bring my people again from the depths of the sea'* (Ps. 68:22)."

Let us commit our ways unto the Lord. Mine is a particularly difficult way, but *"I know that my redeemer liveth"* (Job 19:25), and He will lead me by a right way. He will be our Guide even unto death, and after death He will guide us through those unknown tracks of the mysterious region and will cause us to rest with Him forever.

IN TIMES OF POVERTY

If we are ever in great poverty, or if we are very limited in means for the Lord's work, let us not be afraid that we will never have our needs supplied. Instead, let us cast off such fears as we listen to the music of these words: *"Fear not: for I have redeemed thee."* God Himself looked down from heaven and saw that there was no man who could give Him a ransom for his brother (Ps. 49:7), and each man on his own part was hopelessly bankrupt. Yet, despite our spiritual poverty, He found the means of our redemption. What is the significance of this?

Notice how the Holy Spirit makes use of this fact: *"He that spared not his own Son, but delivered him up for us all, how shall he not with him also freely give us all things?"* (Rom. 8:32). We cannot have a need that the Lord will not supply. Since God has given us Jesus, He will give us, not some things, but *"all things."* Indeed, all things are ours in Christ Jesus. No necessity of life can for a single moment be compared to the fearful necessity that the Lord has already supplied. The infinite gift of God's own Son is far greater than all that can be included in the term *"all things."* Therefore, the poor and needy may take courage that God has said to them, *"Fear not: for I have redeemed thee."* Perplexity and poverty are thus effectively met.

WHEN WE FEEL INSIGNIFICANT

At times we are troubled by a sense of our personal insignificance. It seems too much to hope that God's infinite mind should enter into our lowly affairs. Though David said, *"I am poor and needy; yet the Lord thinketh upon me"* (Ps. 40:17), we are not always quite prepared to say the same. We make our sorrows great under the vain idea that they are too small for the Lord to notice.

I believe that our greatest miseries spring from those little worries that we hesitate to bring to our heavenly Father. Our gracious God puts an end to all such thoughts as these by saying, *"Fear not: for I have redeemed thee."* You are not of such little importance as you suppose. The Lord would never waste His sacred expenditure. He bought you with a price, and therefore He places much confidence in you. Notice what the Lord says: *"Since thou wast precious in my sight, thou hast been honourable, and I have loved thee: therefore will I give men for thee, and people for thy life"* (Isa. 43:4).

It is amazing that the Lord should think so much of us as to give Jesus for us. *"What is man, that thou art mindful of him?"* (Ps. 8:4). Yet God's mind is filled with thoughts of love toward man. Do you not know that His only begotten Son entered this world and became a man? The Man Christ Jesus has a name at which every knee shall bow (Phil. 2:10), and He is so dear to the Father that, for His sake, His chosen ones are accepted and are made to enjoy the freest access to Him. We may truly sing,

> So near, so very near to God,
> Nearer we cannot be,
> For in the person of His Son
> We are as near as He.

The very hairs of our heads are all numbered (Matt. 10:30), and we may roll the least burden upon the Lord. We may cast off the cares that we should not hold on to, for *"he careth for* [us]" (1 Pet. 5:7). He who redeemed us never forgets us. His wounds have *"graven* [us] *upon the palms of* [His] *hands"* (Isa. 49:16) and written our names deep in His side. Jesus stoops to our level, for He stooped to bear the cross to redeem us. Do not, therefore, be afraid because of your insignificance.

[27] *Why sayest thou, O Jacob, and speakest, O Israel, My way is hid from the LORD, and my judgment is passed over from my God?*

> ²⁸ *Hast thou not known? hast thou not heard, that the everlasting God, the LORD, the Creator of the ends of the earth, fainteth not, neither is weary? There is no searching of his understanding.*
> ²⁹ *He giveth power to the faint; and to them that have no might he increaseth strength.* (Isa. 40:27–29)

The Lord remembers the insignificant ones in Israel. He carries the lambs *"in his bosom"* (v. 11).

WHEN WE SENSE OUR FICKLENESS

We are liable to worry a little when we think of our changeableness. If you are at all like me, you are very far from being always the same. I am sometimes lifted up to the very heavens, and then I go down to the deeps. I am at one time bright with joy and confidence, and at another time dark as midnight with doubts and fears. Even Elijah, who was so brave, had his fainting fits. We are to be blamed for this, and yet the fact remains: our experience is like an April day, when rain and sunshine take turns. Amid our mournful changes, we rejoice to hear the Lord's own voice saying, *"Fear not: for I have redeemed thee."* Everything is not shifting waves; there is rock somewhere. Redemption is an accomplished fact. "The Cross, it stands fast. Hallelujah!"

The price has been paid, the ransom accepted. This has been accomplished and can never be undone. Jesus says, *"I have redeemed thee."* Our feelings may change, but this does not alter the fact that we have been bought with a price and made the Lord's own by the precious blood of Jesus. The Lord God has already done so much for us that our salvation is sure in Christ Jesus. Will He begin to build, and fail to finish? Will He lay the foundation in the everlasting covenant, dedicate the walls with the infinite sacrifice of the Lamb of God, give up the choicest Treasure He ever had, the chosen and precious One of God, to be the Cornerstone and then not finish the work He has begun? No, if He has redeemed us, He has, in that act, given us the pledge of all things.

See how the gifts of God are tied to this redemption. *"I have redeemed thee, I have called thee"* (Isa. 43:1).

> [29] *For whom he did foreknow, he also did predestinate to be conformed to the image of his Son, that he might be the firstborn among many brethren.*
> [30] *Moreover whom he did predestinate, them he also called: and whom he called, them he also justified: and whom he justified, them he also glorified.*
> *(Rom. 8:29–30)*

THE PROMISE OF REDEMPTION

Here is a chain in which each link is joined to all the rest, so that they cannot be separated. If God had only gone so far as to make a promise, He would not have gone back on it. If God had only gone so far as to swear an oath by Himself, He would not have failed to keep it. But because He went beyond promise and oath, and by this the Sacrifice was slain and the covenant was ratified, it would be blasphemous to imagine that He would afterward annul His commitment and turn from His solemn pledge. God never goes back on His promises, and consequently His redemption will redeem, and in redeeming it will secure all things for us. *"Who shall separate us from the love of Christ?"* (Rom. 8:35).

With the bloodstain upon us, we may well cease to fear. How can we perish? How can we be deserted in the hour of need? We have been bought with too great a price for our Redeemer to let us slip. Therefore, let us march on with confidence, hearing our Redeemer say to us,

> ² *When thou passest through the waters, I will be with thee; and through the rivers, they shall not overflow thee: when thou walkest through the fire, thou shalt not be burned; neither shall the flame kindle upon thee.* *(Isa. 43:2)*

Concerning His redeemed, the Lord will say to the Enemy, *"Touch not mine anointed, and do my prophets no harm"* (1 Chron. 16:22). *"The stars in their courses"* (Judg. 5:20) fight for the ransomed of the Lord. If their eyes were opened, they would see the *"mountain...full of horses and chariots of fire round about* [them]" (2 Kings 6:17).

Oh, how my weary heart prizes redeeming love! If it were not for this, I would lie down and die. Friends forsake me, foes surround me, I am filled with contempt and tortured with subtlety and cunning that I cannot defeat. But, as the Lord of all brought our Lord Jesus back from the dead by the blood of the everlasting covenant, so by the blood of His covenant does He loose His prisoners and sustain the hearts of those who tremble at His Word. *"O my soul, thou hast trodden down strength"* (Judg. 5:21), for the Lord has said to you, *"Fear not: for I have redeemed thee."*

Chapter 9

Bonds of Unity

I drew them with cords of a man,
with bands of love: and I was to them
as they that take off the yoke on their jaws,
and I laid meat unto them.
—Hosea 11:4

Systematic theologians have usually agreed that there are three aspects of union with Christ: natural, spiritual, and covenantal. It is possible that these three terms are comprehensive enough to cover the whole subject, but I know of two other ways in which we are united with Christ. These are the bond of love and the bond of purpose, and I will mention them before the other three.

THE BOND OF LOVE

From the beginning, believers were joined to Christ by bonds of everlasting love. Before He took their nature upon Himself or brought them into a conscious enjoyment of Himself, His heart was set on them, and His soul delighted in them. Long before the worlds were made,

His omniscient eye beheld His chosen ones and viewed them with delight. Strong were the indissoluble bonds of love which then united Jesus to the souls whom He determined to redeem. No bars of steel could have been more real and effective bonds.

True love, of all things in the universe, has the greatest cementing force and will bear the greatest strain. Indeed, love will endure the heaviest pressure. Who can tell what trials the Savior's love has borne and how well such love has endured them? No union was ever truer than this. As the soul of Jonathan was knit to the soul of David so that he loved David as his own soul, so was our glorious Lord united and joined to us by ties of fervent, faithful love. Love has a most potent power in creating and sustaining unity, but it never displays its force as well as when it brings the Creator into oneness with the created, the divine into alliance with the human. This, then, is to be regarded as the day-spring of union—the love of Christ embracing in its folds the whole of the elected family of God.

THE BOND OF PURPOSE

There is, moreover, a union of purpose as well as of love. In the union of love, the elect are made one with Jesus by the act and will of the Son. In the union of purpose, they are joined to Him by the ordination and decree of the Father. These divine acts are equally eternal. The Son loved and chose His people to be His own bride; the Father made the same choice and decreed that the chosen ones would be forever one with His all-glorious Son. The Son loved them, and the Father decreed them His portion and inheritance; the Father ordained them to be what the Son Himself had made them.

In God's purpose, His people have been eternally associated with Christ as parts of one plan. Salvation was the foreordained scheme by which God magnified Himself, and it was necessary that a Savior was in that plan—someone associated with the people chosen to be saved. The scope of redemption included both Redeemer and redeemed. They could not be dissociated in the mind and will of the all-planning Jehovah.

The same Book that contains the names of the heirs of life also contains the name of their Redeemer. Jesus could not have been a Redeemer unless souls had been given Him to redeem, nor could believers have been called the ransomed of the Lord if He had not undertaken to purchase them. Redemption, when decided upon by the God of heaven, included in it both Christ and His people; therefore, in the decree that established it, they were brought into a near and intimate alliance.

God foresaw the catastrophe of the Fall, and this foresight led Him to provide a gracious way for the elect to escape their inevitable ruin. Thus, other forms of union followed as part of the divine arrangement. These forms of union, besides their immediate purpose in salvation, undoubtedly had a further purpose of illustrating the condescending alliance that Jesus had formed with His chosen. The following are these other forms of union.

UNDER THE COVENANT

Jesus is one with His elect through a covenant bond. Every heir of flesh and blood has a personal interest in Adam because he was the covenant head and the representative of the race under the law of works. Under the law of grace, however, every redeemed soul is one with the Lord from heaven, since He is the Second Adam, the

Sponsor and Substitute of the elect in the new covenant
of love.

The writer of Hebrews declared that Levi was in the
loins of Abraham when Melchizedek met him (Heb. 7:9–
10). It is equally true that the believer was in the loins of
Jesus Christ, the Mediator, when the covenant settle-
ments of grace were decreed, ratified, and made sure forever. Thus, whatever Christ has done, He has done for
the whole body of His church. We were crucified in Him
and buried with Him (Col. 2:10), and to make it still
more wonderful, we are risen with Him and have even
ascended with Him to heavenly places (Eph. 2:6).

In this way, the church has fulfilled the law and is
"accepted in the beloved" (Eph. 1:6). It is thus that she is
regarded with satisfaction by the just Jehovah, for He
views her in Jesus and does not look upon her as separate from her covenant Head. As the anointed Redeemer
of Israel, Christ Jesus has nothing distinct from His
church, but all that He has He holds for her.

Adam's righteousness was ours as long as he maintained it, and his sin was ours the moment he committed
it. In the same manner, all that the Second Adam is, or
does, is ours as well as His, seeing that He is our Representative. Here is the foundation of the covenant of
grace. This gracious system of representation and substitution, which moved Justin Martyr to cry out, "O blessed
change! O sweet permutation!" is the very groundwork
of the Gospel of our salvation and is to be received with
strong faith and rapturous joy. In every place, believers
are perfectly one with Jesus.

UNITED IN OUR NATURES

For the accomplishment of the great works of
atonement and perfect obedience, it was necessary that

the Lord Jesus should take upon Himself *"the likeness of sinful flesh"* (Rom. 8:3). Thus, He became one with us in our nature, for in Holy Scripture all partakers of flesh and blood are regarded as of one family. By the fact of common descent from Adam, all men are of one race, seeing that God *"hath made of one blood all nations of men for to dwell on all the face of the earth"* (Acts 17:26). Hence, in the Bible, man is spoken of universally as *"thy brother"* (Lev. 19:17) and *"thy neighbour"* (Exod. 20:16), to whom, because of our nature and descent, we are required to render kindness and goodwill.

Now, our Great Melchizedek, in His divinity, is *"without father, without mother, without descent, having neither beginning of days, nor end of life"* (Heb. 7:3). He is at an infinite distance from fallen manhood both in essence and in rank. Yet, as to His manhood, He is to be reckoned as one of us. He was born of a woman. He hung upon her breasts and was gently bounced upon her knee. He grew from infancy to youth and then to manhood, and in every stage He was a true and real partaker of our humanity. He is as truly of the race of Adam as He is divine.

Jesus is God without fiction or metaphor, and He is man beyond doubt or dispute. In Christ, the Godhead was not humanized and thereby diluted, and manhood was not transformed into divinity and thereby made more than human. No man was ever more completely human than was the Son of Man, the Man of Sorrows, and the One who was acquainted with grief. He is man's Brother, for He bore the whole nature of man. *"The Word was made flesh, and dwelt among us"* (John 1:14). He who was Very God of Very God made Himself *"a little lower than the angels"* (Ps. 8:5), and *"took upon him the form of a servant, and was made in the likeness of men"* (Phil. 2:7).

This was done with the most excellent intentions with regard to our redemption, inasmuch as it was necessary that man should suffer because he had sinned. However, it undoubtedly had a further purpose: to honor the church and to enable her Lord to sympathize with her. The apostle very beautifully remarked,

> ¹⁴ *Forasmuch then as the children are partakers of flesh and blood, he also himself likewise took part of the same; that through death he might destroy him that had the power of death, that is, the devil;*
> ¹⁵ *and deliver them who through fear of death were all their lifetime subject to bondage.*   *(Heb. 2:14–15)*

He also wrote, *"For we have not an high priest which cannot be touched with the feeling of our infirmities; but was in all points tempted like as we are, yet without sin"* (Heb. 4:15).

Thus, in ties of blood, Jesus, the Son of Man, is one with all the heirs of heaven, *"for which cause he is not ashamed to call them brethren"* (Heb. 2:11). Here we have reason for the strongest comfort and delight, seeing that *"both he that sanctifieth and they who are sanctified are all of one"* (v. 11). We can say of our Lord as poor Naomi said of bounteous Boaz, *"The man is near of kin unto us, one of our next kinsmen"* (Ruth 2:20). Overwhelmed by the liberality of our blessed Lord, we are often led to cry with Ruth, *"Why have I found grace in thine eyes, that thou shouldest take knowledge of me, seeing I am a stranger?"* (v. 10). Are we not ready to die with wonder when, in answer to such a question, He tells us that He is our Brother, bone of our bones and flesh of our flesh?

If in all our trials and distresses we would always treasure in our minds the remembrance of our Redeemer's manhood, we would never bemoan the absence

118

of a sympathizing heart. We would always have His abundant compassion to comfort us. He is no stranger; He is able to enter into the heart's bitterness, for He Himself has tasted bitter hardships. Let us never doubt His power to sympathize with us in our infirmities and sorrows.

There is one aspect of this subject of our natural union with Christ that it would be improper to pass over, for it is very precious to the believer. While the Lord Jesus takes upon Himself our nature (Phil. 2:7), He restores in us the image of God that was stained and defaced by the fall of Adam (2 Pet. 1:4). He raises us from the degradation of sin to the dignity of perfection. Thus, in a twofold sense, the Head and members are of one nature, and not like the monstrous image that Nebuchadnezzar saw in his dream, where the head was of fine gold, but the belly and the thighs were of brass; the legs of iron, and the feet part iron and part clay. (See Daniel 2:32–33.)

Christ's body is no absurd combination of opposites; the Head is immortal, and the body is immortal, too, for thus the record stands: *"Because I live, ye shall live also"* (John 14:19). *"As is the heavenly, such are they also that are heavenly. And as we have borne the image of the earthy, we shall also bear the image of the heavenly"* (1 Cor. 15:48–49). In just a short time, this will be more fully manifested to us, for *"this corruptible must put on incorruption, and this mortal must put on immortality"* (v. 53).

Whatever the Head is, such is the body and every member in particular—a chosen Head and chosen members, an accepted Head and accepted members, a living Head and living members. If the Head is of pure gold, all the parts of the body are also of pure gold. Thus, the union of our human nature with Christ's divine nature is twofold—a perfect basis for the closest communion.

Stop here for a moment and contemplate the infinite condescension of the Son of God in lifting your wretchedness into blessed union with His glory. You cannot think of these things without ecstatic amazement. You are so lowly that, in remembrance of your mortality, you may say to corruption, *"Thou art my father: to the worm, Thou art my mother, and my sister"* (Job 17:14). Yet, in Christ, you are so honored that you can say to the Almighty, *"Abba, Father"* (Rom. 8:15), and to the Incarnate God, "You are my Brother and my Husband."

If being descendants of ancient and noble families makes men think highly of themselves, surely we have reason to glory over the heads of them all. Lay hold of this privilege; do not let a senseless laziness make you neglect to trace this lineage. Do not allow any foolish attachment to present vanities occupy your thoughts to the point that this glorious privilege is excluded. We have the heavenly honor of union with Christ.

We must now retrace our steps to the ancient mountains and contemplate our union with Christ in one of its earliest forms.

Spiritual Unity

Christ Jesus is also joined to His people in a spiritual union. Borrowing once more from the story of Ruth, we notice that Boaz, although one with Ruth by kinship, did not rest until he had entered into an even closer union with her, namely, that of marriage. In the same manner, added to the natural union of Christ with His people, there is a spiritual union by which He assumes the position of Husband, while the church is His bride.

In love, Christ espoused the church to Himself, as a chaste virgin, long before she fell under the yoke of

bondage. Full of burning affection, He toiled as Jacob did
for Rachel, until she had been paid for in full. And now,
having sought her by His Spirit and having brought her
to know and love Him, He awaits the glorious hour when
their mutual bliss will be consummated at the Marriage
Supper of the Lamb.

The glorious Bridegroom has not yet presented His
betrothed, perfected and complete, before the Majesty of
heaven. She has not yet actually entered into the enjoyment of her dignities as His wife and queen. Instead, she
is still a wanderer in a world of woe, a dweller in the
tents of Kedar (Ps. 120:5). But even now she is the bride,
the spouse of Jesus, dear to His heart, precious in His
sight, and united with His person. In love and tenderness, He says to her,

> Forget thee I will not, I cannot, thy name
> Engraved on My heart doth for ever remain:
> The palms of My hands whilst I look on I see
> The wounds I received when suffering for thee.

Toward the church, Christ exercises all the affec-
tionate roles of Husband. He makes rich provision for
her needs, pays all her debts, allows her to assume His
name and to share in all His wealth. He will never act
otherwise to her. He will never mention the word *di-
vorce*, for *"he hateth putting away"* (Mal. 2:16). Death
severs the conjugal tie between the most loving mortals,
but it cannot divide the links of this immortal marriage.

In heaven no one marries, but everyone is as an angel of God; yet there is one marvelous exception to the
rule, for in heaven Christ and His church will celebrate
their joyous nuptials. This marriage relationship, as it is
more lasting, is also more intimate than earthly wedlock.
Even the purest and most fervent love of a husband is

but a faint picture of the flame that burns in the heart of Jesus. Surpassing all human union is that spiritual cleaving unto the church for which Christ left His Father and became one flesh with her.

If this is the union that abides between our souls and the person of our Lord, how deep and broad is the channel of our communion! This is no narrow pipe through which a threadlike stream may wind its way! No, it is a channel of amazing depth and breadth, along which a substantial volume of living water may roll its strength. Behold, He has set before us an open door; let us not be slow to enter. The city of communion has many pearly gates. Every other gate is made up of one pearl, and each gate is thrown open to the uttermost so that we may enter, assured of welcome.

If there were only one small opening through which we could talk with Jesus, it would be a high privilege to thrust a word of fellowship through that narrow door. Indeed, we are blessed in having so large an entrance! If the Lord Jesus had been far away from us, with many a stormy sea between, we would have longed to send a messenger to Him to carry Him our love and to bring us news from His Father's house. But, see His kindness! He has built His house next door to ours. More than that, He settles in with us, and He resides in our poor humble hearts, so that He may have perpetual communion with us.

Oh, how foolish must we be, if we do not live in habitual communion with Him! When the road is long and dangerous and difficult, we do not wonder that friends seldom meet with each other. But when friends live together, when they have the sort of friendship that was between Jonathan and David, will they forget about each other? A wife may, when her husband is on a journey, spend many days without conversing with him. But she could never endure to be separated from him in this manner if she knew that he was still in one of the rooms of their own house. Seek your Lord, for He is near; embrace Him, for He is your Brother; hold Him fast, for He is your Husband; press Him to your heart, for He is of your own flesh.

VITAL UNION

So far in this chapter, we have only considered the acts of Christ for us, by which He proves His union to us and brings it into effect. We must now come to more personal and tangible forms of this great truth.

Those who are set apart for the Lord are in due time severed from the impure mass of fallen humanity. By sovereign grace, they are engrafted into the person of the Lord Jesus. This, which we call vital union, is a matter of experience rather than of doctrine. It must be learned in the heart, not by the head.

Like every other work of the Spirit, the actual implantation of the soul into Christ Jesus is a mysterious and secret operation. It cannot be understood by carnal reason any more than the new birth can be understood, and the two experiences accompany one another. Nevertheless, the spiritual man discerns it as a most essential thing in the salvation of the soul, and he clearly sees how a living union with Christ is the certain result of the quickening influence of the Holy Spirit. Indeed, in some respects, this living union is identical with the influence of the Spirit.

When, in His mercy, the Lord passed by and saw us in our natural, guilt-ridden state, He first of all said, "Live." He did this first because, without life, there can be no spiritual knowledge, feeling, or motion. Life is one of the absolutely essential things in spiritual matters, and until it is bestowed, we are incapable of partaking in the things of the kingdom.

Now, the life that grace confers upon believers at the moment of their renewal is none other than the life of Christ, which, like the sap from the stem, runs into us, the branches, and establishes a living connection between our souls and Jesus. Faith is the grace that perceives this union and proceeds from it as its first fruit. To use a metaphor, it is the neck that joins the body of the church to its all-glorious Head.

Faith lays hold of the Lord Jesus with a firm and determined grasp. She knows His excellence and worth, and no temptation can induce her to put her trust elsewhere. In turn, Christ Jesus is so delighted with this heavenly grace that He never ceases to strengthen and sustain her by the loving embrace and all-sufficient support of His eternal arms. Here, then, is established a living, tangible, and delightful union, which casts forth streams of love, confidence, sympathy, satisfaction, and joy, from which both the bride and Bridegroom love to drink.

When the eye is clear and the soul can perceive this oneness between itself and Christ, it is as if redeemed and Redeemer share the same pulse, or as if the same blood flows through their veins together. Then the heart is made exceedingly glad; it is as near to heaven as it ever can be on earth, and it is prepared for the enjoyment of the most sublime and spiritual kind of fellowship. This union may be quite as true when we are troubled with doubts concerning it, but it cannot offer consolation to the soul unless it is indisputably proven and assuredly felt. At such a time, it is indeed a honeycomb dripping with sweetness, a precious jewel sparkling with light.

Chapter 10

"I Will Give You Rest"

*Come unto me, all ye that labour and are
heavy laden, and I will give you rest.*
—Matthew 11:28

These words are typically considered as an encouragement to those who labor and are burdened. Therefore, we may have failed to read them as a promise for ourselves. But, beloved friends, we have come to Jesus, and therefore He stands committed to fulfill this priceless pledge to us. We may now enjoy the promise, for we have obeyed the precept. The faithful and true Witness, whose word is truth, promised us rest if we would come to Him. Therefore, since we have come to Him and are always coming to Him, we may boldly say, "O God, who is our Peace, make good Your word to us in which you have said, *'I will give you rest.'*"

By faith, we hear our Lord saying to each of us, with a voice of the sweetest music, *"I will give you rest."* May the Holy Spirit bring to each of us the fullness of the rest and peace of God as we consider the promise in these words.

A Promise for Our Spiritual Natures

While studying the Scriptures, we need holy insight to read between the lines and beneath the letter of the Word. We must be enabled by the Holy Spirit to see the deeper meaning to a promise such as, *"I will give you rest."* This promise must mean rest to all parts of our spiritual natures. Our bodies cannot rest if our heads are aching or if our feet are full of pain; if one part of us is disturbed, our bodies are unable to rest. Likewise, the higher nature is one. All its faculties and powers are bound together by such intimate sympathies that every one of them must rest or none can be at ease. But Jesus gives real and universal rest to every part of our spiritual beings.

For the Heart

The heart is by nature as restless as the ocean's waves. It seeks an object for its affection, and when it finds one beneath the stars, it is doomed to sorrow. Either the beloved changes and there is disappointment, or death comes in and there is bereavement. The more tender the heart, the greater its unrest. For some people, the heart is simply the strongest muscle, and these individuals remain undisturbed, because they are callous. But the sensitive, the generous, the unselfish, are often found *"seeking rest, and find*[ing] *none"* (Matt. 12:43). To such individuals, the Lord Jesus says, *"Come unto me...and I will give you rest."*

Look here, you loving ones, for here is a refuge for your wounded love! You may delight yourselves in the Well Beloved and never fear that He will fail or forget you. Love will not be wasted, however much it may be lavished upon Jesus. He deserves it all, and He requites it all. In loving Him, the heart finds a delicious contentment. When the head rests on His chest, it enjoys an ease that no down-filled pillow could bestow. Madame Guyon rested amid severe persecutions, because her great love for Jesus filled her soul to the brim! O aching heart, come here, for Jesus says, *"I will give you rest."*

For the Conscience

The conscience, when it is at all alive and awake, is much disturbed when the holy law of God has been broken by sin. As you know, once the conscience is aroused, it is not easily quieted. Neither unbelief nor superstition can lull it to sleep; it defies these opiates of falsehood and worries the soul with perpetual annoyance. Like the troubled sea, it cannot rest, but it constantly casts the mire and dirt of past transgressions and iniquities upon the shore of memory.

Is this your situation? Then Jesus says, *"I will give you rest."* If fears and anxieties arise at any time from an awakened conscience, they can only be safely and surely quieted when we run to the Crucified One. In the blessed truth of Christ's substitutionary death, which is acceptable to God and has been fully accomplished by the Lord Jesus, our minds find peace. Justice is honored and law is vindicated in the sacrifice of Christ.

Since God is satisfied, I may be satisfied, too. Since the Father has raised Jesus from the dead and has set Him at His own right hand, there can be no question about His acceptance. Consequently, all who are in Him are accepted also. We are under no fear now of being condemned; Jesus gives us rest by enabling us to put forth the challenge, *"Who is he that condemneth?"* (Rom.

8:34), and to give the reassuring answer, *"It is Christ that died"* (v. 34).

For the Intellect

The intellect is another source of unrest, and in these times there are many things that attempt to trouble the mind. Doubts, stinging like the bites of mosquitoes, are suggested by almost every page of the literature of the day. Most men are drifting like vessels that have no anchors, and they come into collision with us. How can we rest? One scheme of philosophy eats up the other; each new form of heresy devours the last. Is there any foundation? Is anything true? Or is it all fairy tale, and are we doomed to be the victims of an ever changing lie?

O soul, do not seek an answer to this by learning of men, but come and learn of Jesus, and you will find rest! Believe Jesus, and let all the rabbis contradict you if they must. The Son of God was made flesh; He lived, He died, He rose again, He lives, He loves. This is true, and all that He teaches in His Word is assured truth. The rest may blow away like chaff before the wind. A mind in pursuit of truth is a dove without a proper resting place, until it finds its rest in Jesus.

Concerning All Things

Next, these words mean rest about all things. The person who is uneasy about anything has not found rest. A thousand thorns and briars grow on the soil of this earth, and no man can happily walk life's way unless his feet are *"shod with the preparation of the gospel of peace"* (Eph. 6:15), which Jesus gives. In Christ, we are at rest concerning our duties, for He instructs and helps us in them. In Him, we are at rest about our trials, for He sympathizes with us in them. With His love, we are at rest as to the movements of Providence, for His Father loves us and will not allow anything to harm us. Concerning the past, we rest in His forgiving love. As to the present, it is bright with His loving fellowship. As to the future, it is brilliant with His expected coming.

This is true of the little things as well as the great. He who saves us from the battle-ax of satanic temptation also extracts the thorn of a domestic trial. We may rest in Jesus concerning our sick child, our business trouble, or grief of any kind. He is our Comforter in all things, our Sympathizer in every form of temptation. Do you have this all-covering rest? If not, why not? Jesus gives it; why do you not partake of it? Do you have something that you could not bring to Him? Then flee from it, for it is not a fit thing for a believer to possess. A disciple should know neither grief nor joy that he could not reveal to his Lord.

This rest must be a very wonderful one, since Jesus gives it. He does not give by ounces and pounds. Instead, He gives golden gifts in immeasurable quantities. It is Jesus who gives *"the peace of God, which passeth all understanding"* (Phil. 4:7). It is written, *"Great peace have they which love thy law"* (Ps. 119:165); what peace must they have who love God's Son! There are times when Jesus gives us a heavenly paradise of rest; we cannot describe the divine repose of our hearts at such times.

We read in the Gospels that when Jesus hushed the storm, *"there was a great calm"* (Matt. 8:26)—not simply "a calm," but a great calm—unusual, absolute, perfect, memorable. It reminds us of the stillness that John described in the book of Revelation: *"I saw four angels standing on the four corners of the earth, holding the four winds of the earth, that the wind should not blow on the earth, nor on the sea, nor on any tree"* (Rev. 7:1). Not a ripple stirred the waters, not a leaf moved on the trees.

Assuredly, our Lord has given a blessed rest to those who trust Him and follow Him. They are often unable to inform others as to the depths of their peace and the reasons upon which it is founded. But they know it, and it brings them an inward wealth that causes the fortune of an ungodly millionaire to appear to be poverty itself. May all of us, by happy, personal experience, know to the fullest the meaning of our Savior's promise, *"I will give you rest"*!

But now, in the second place, let us ask, "Why should we have this rest?"

WHY WE SHOULD HAVE THIS REST

Jesus Gives It

The first answer is in our text. We should enjoy this rest because Jesus gives it. Since He gives it, we ought to take it. Because He gives it, we may take it. I have known some Christians who have thought that it would be presumptuous on their part to take this rest, so they have kept fluttering about like frightened birds, weary from their long flights but not daring to fold their tired wings and rest. If there is any presumption in the case, let us not be so presumptuous as to think that we know better than our Lord. He gives us rest. For that reason, if for no other, let us take it promptly and gratefully. *"Rest in the LORD, and wait patiently for him"* (Ps. 37:7). Say with David, *"My heart is fixed, O God, my heart is fixed: I will sing and give praise"* (Ps. 57:7).

It Will Refresh Us

Next, we should take the rest that Jesus gives because it will refresh us. We are often weary; sometimes we are weary *in* God's work, though I trust we are never weary *of* it. There are many things that cause us weariness: sin, sorrow, the worldliness of some who say they believe, the prevalence of error in the church, and so on. Often we are like a tired child who can hold up his little head no longer. What does he do? Why, he just goes to sleep in his mother's arms! Let us be as wise as the little one, and let us rest in our loving Savior's embrace.

One poet wrote of "tired nature's sweet restorer, balmy sleep," and so it is. Sometimes the very best thing a Christian can do is, literally, to go to sleep. When he wakes, he will be so refreshed that he will seem to be in a new world. But, spiritually, there is no refreshment like that which comes from the rest that Christ gives. As Isaiah said, *"This is the rest wherewith ye may cause the weary to rest; and this is the refreshing"* (Isa. 28:12).

Dr. Bonar's sweet hymn, which is so suitable for a sinner coming to Christ for the first time, is equally appropriate for a weary believer returning to his Savior's arms. The weary Christian, too, can sing,

> I heard the voice of Jesus say,
>   "Come unto Me, and rest;
> Lay down, thou weary one, lay down
>   Thy head upon My breast."
> I came to Jesus as I was,
>   Weary, and worn, and sad:
> I found in Him a resting-place,
>   And He has made me glad.

It Improves Our Focus

Another reason why we should have this rest is that it will enable us to concentrate all our faculties on the highest purpose. Many, who might be strong servants of the Lord, are very weak because their energies are not concentrated on one purpose. They do not say with Paul, *"This one thing I do"* (Phil. 3:13). We are such poor creatures that we often cannot occupy our minds with more than one subject at a time. Why, even the buzzing of a fly or the bite of a mosquito would be quite sufficient to take our thoughts away from our present holy service! As long as we have any burden weighing on our shoulders, we cannot enjoy perfect rest; and as long as there is any burden on our consciences or our hearts, our souls cannot rest.

How are we to be freed from these burdens? Only by yielding ourselves wholly to the Great Burden-Bearer, who says, *"Come unto me...and I will give you rest."* When we possess this rest, all our faculties will be centered and focused on one objective, and with undivided hearts we will seek God's glory.

We Will Testify for Him

When we have obtained this rest, we will also be able to testify for our Lord. I remember, when I first began to teach Sunday school, that one day I was speaking to my class upon the words, *"He that believeth on me hath everlasting life"* (John 6:47). I was rather taken by surprise when one of the boys said to me, "Teacher, do you have everlasting life?" I replied, "I hope so." The student was not satisfied with my answer, so he asked another question, "But, teacher, don't you know?"

The boy was right; there can be no true testimony except one that springs from assured conviction of our own safety and joy in the Lord. We speak what we know; we believe and therefore speak. Rest of the heart, which we receive through coming to Christ, enables us to invite others to Him with great confidence, for we can tell them what heavenly peace He has given to us. This will enable us to put the Gospel in a very attractive light, for the evidence of our own experience will help others to trust the Lord for themselves. With the beloved apostle John, we will be able to say to our hearers,

> [1] *That which was from the beginning, which we have heard, which we have seen with our eyes, which we have looked upon, and our hands have handled, of the Word of life;*
> [2] *(for the life was manifested, and we have seen it, and bear witness, and show unto you that eternal life, which was with the Father, and was manifested unto us;)*
> [3] *that which we have seen and heard declare we unto you, that ye also may have fellowship with us: and truly our fellowship is with the Father, and with his Son Jesus Christ.*   *(1 John 1:1–3)*

It Is Necessary for Growth

In addition, this rest is necessary for our growth. The lily in the garden is not taken up and transplanted two or three times a day; that would be the way to prevent all growth. Rather, it is kept in one place and tenderly nurtured. It is by keeping it quite still that the gardener helps it to reach perfection. A child of God would grow much more rapidly if he would simply rest in one place instead of always being on the move. *"In returning and rest shall ye be saved; in quietness and in confidence shall be your strength"* (Isa. 30:15). Martha was burdened with preparing the meal, but Mary sat at Jesus' feet. It is not difficult to tell which of them was more likely to grow in the grace and knowledge of our Lord Jesus Christ.

It Prepares Us for Heaven

There is another reason why we must have this rest that Christ gives: it will prepare us for heaven. I was reading a book the other day in which I found this expression: "The streets of heaven begin on earth." That is true; heaven is not as far away as some people think. Heaven is the place of perfect holiness, the place of sinless service, the place of eternal glory, and there is nothing that will prepare us for heaven like this rest that Jesus gives. Heaven must be in us before we are in heaven, and the person who has this rest has begun his heaven below.

Enoch was virtually in heaven while he walked with God on the earth, and he had only to continue that holy walk to find himself actually in heaven. This world is part of our Lord's great house, of which heaven is the upper story. Some of us may hear the Master's call, "Come up higher," sooner than we think. Then, as we rest *in* Christ, we will rest *with* Christ. The more we have of this blessed rest now, the better we will be prepared for the rest that remains for the people of God, that eternal keeping of a Sabbath in the paradise above (Heb. 4:9–10).

How to Obtain This Rest

By Coming to Christ

Now, how can we obtain this rest? First, we obtain the rest of Christ by coming to Him. He says, *"Come unto me...and I will give you rest."* I trust that you, my reader, have come to Christ by faith; now prepare yourself for blessed fellowship and communion with Him. Keep on coming to Him, continually coming and never going away.

When you wake up in the morning, come to Christ in an act of renewed communion with Him. All day long, keep on coming to Him even while you are occupied with the affairs of this life. And at night, let your last waking moments be spent in coming to Jesus. Come to Christ by searching the Scriptures, for you will find Him there on almost every page. Come to Christ in your thoughts, desires, aspirations, and wishes. In this way, the promise of the text will be fulfilled for you: *"I will give you rest."*

By Yielding to Christ

Next, we obtain rest by yielding to Christ. *"Take my yoke upon you...and ye shall find rest unto your souls"* (Matt. 11:29). Christ calls us to wear His yoke, not to make one for ourselves. He wants us to share the yoke with Him, to be His true yokefellows. It is wonderful that He is willing to be yoked with us; the only greater wonder is that we are so unwilling to be yoked with Him. When we take His yoke upon us, what joy we will have in our eternal rest!

Here we find rest for our souls, a further rest beyond that which He gives us when we come to Him. We first rest in Jesus by faith, and then we rest in Him by obedience. The first rest He gives through His death; the further rest we find through imitating His life.

By Learning of Christ

Lastly, we secure this rest by learning of Christ. *"Learn of me; for I am meek and lowly in heart: and ye shall find rest unto your souls"* (Matt. 11:29). We are to be workers with Christ, taking His yoke upon us. At the same time, we are to be students in Christ's school, learning of Him. We are to learn of Christ, and to learn Christ; He is both the Teacher and the Lesson. His gentleness of heart makes Him fit to teach and makes Him the best illustration of His own teaching. If we can become like Him, we will rest as He does. The *"lowly in heart"* will have restful hearts. May we find that full rest, for the Great Rest-Giver's sake! Amen.

Chapter 11

Jesus Asleep
on a Pillow

And he was in the hinder part of the ship,
asleep on a pillow: and they awake him,
and say unto him, Master, carest thou not
that we perish? And he arose, and rebuked
the wind, and said unto the sea,
Peace, be still. And the wind ceased,
and there was a great calm.
—Mark 4:38–39

Our Lord took His disciples with Him into the ship to teach them a practical lesson. It is one thing to talk to people about our oneness with them, about how they should exercise faith in time of danger, and about their real safety in apparent peril. But it is another and far better thing to go into the ship with them, to let them feel all the terror of the storm, and then to arise and rebuke the wind and say to the sea, *"Peace, be still."* Our Lord gave His disciples a kind of school lesson, an acted sermon, in which the truth was set forth visibly before them. Such teaching produced a wonderful effect on their lives. May we also be instructed by it!

In our text there are two great calms. The first is the calm in the Savior's heart. The second is the calm that He created, through His words, upon the storm-tossed sea.

THE CALMNESS OF OUR LORD

Within the Lord there was a great calm, and that is why there was soon a great calm around Him. What is in God comes out of God. Since there was a calm in Christ for Himself, there was afterward a calm outside for others. What a wonderful inner calm it was! *"He was in the hinder part of the ship, asleep on a pillow."*

Perfect Confidence in God

He had perfect confidence in God that all was well. The waves might roar, the winds might rage, but He was not at all disquieted by their fury. He knew that the waters were in the hollow of His Father's hand, and that every wind was but the breath of His Father's mouth. Therefore, He was not troubled; indeed, He did not have even a thought of concern, for He was as much at ease as He would have been on a sunny day.

His mind and heart were free from every kind of care, for amid the gathering tempest He deliberately lay down and slept like a weary child. He went to the back of the ship, farthest from the spray. He took a pillow and put it under His head, and with definite purpose He fell asleep.

It was His own decision to go to sleep in the storm; He had no reason to stay awake, so pure and perfect was

His confidence in the great Father. What an example this is to us! We do not have half the confidence in God that we ought to have—not even the best of us. The Lord deserves our limitless belief, our unquestioning confidence, our undisturbed reliance. Oh, if only we gave these to Him as the Savior did!

Confidence in His Sonship

Along with His faith in the Father, Jesus also had a sweet confidence in His own Sonship. He did not doubt that He was the Son of the Highest. I may not question God's power to deliver, but I may sometimes question my right to expect deliverance. When I do question it, my comfort vanishes. Our Lord had no doubts of this kind. He had long before heard that word, *"This is my beloved Son, in whom I am well pleased"* (Matt. 3:17). He had lived and walked with God in such a way that the witness within Him was continuous; therefore, He had no question about the Father's love for Him as His own Son. His Father was keeping watch over Him—what better thing could a child do than go to sleep in such a happy position? This is what Jesus did.

You and I, too, need to have a greater assurance of our sonship if we wish to have greater peace with God. The Devil knows this, and so he will come to us with his insinuating suggestion, as he did with Jesus, "If you really are a child of God...." (See Matthew 4:3.) If we have the Spirit of adoption in us, we will put the Accuser to rout at once. The witness of the Holy Spirit within us, that *"we are the children of God"* (Rom. 8:16), will counteract his insinuation. Then we will be filled with a great calm because we will have confidence in our Father and assurance of our sonship.

Leaving Everything with God

Then this blessed Lord of ours had a sweet way of leaving everything with God. He did not stay awake, He did not worry, but He went to sleep. Whatever came, He had left everything in the hands of the great Caretaker. What more is needed? If a watchman were hired to guard my house, I would be foolish if I also sat up for fear of thieves. Why have a watchman if I cannot trust him to watch? *"Cast thy burden upon the LORD"* (Ps. 55:22), but when you have done so, leave it with the Lord and do not try to carry it yourself. Otherwise, you mock God; you use the name of God, but not the reality of God. Lay down every care, even as Jesus did when He went calmly to the rear part of the ship, quietly took a pillow, and went to sleep.

Some of you may say, "I could do that if my cares were solely for myself." You feel that you cannot cast upon God your burden of concern about your children. But your Lord trusted the Father with those dear to Him. Do you not think that Christ's disciples were as precious to Him as our children are to us? If that ship had been wrecked, what would have become of Peter? What would have become of John, *"that disciple whom Jesus loved"* (John 21:7)? Our Lord regarded with intense affection those whom He had chosen and called, and who had been with Him in His temptation. Even so, He was quite content to leave them all in the care of His Father and go to sleep.

You answer, "Yes, but I am obliged to care, whether I want to or not." Is your case, then, more trying than your Lord's? Do you forget that *"there were also with him* [many] *other little ships"* (Mark 4:36)? When the storm was tossing His ship, their little ships were even

more in jeopardy, and He cared for them all. He was the
Lord High Admiral of the Lake of Gennesaret that night.
The other ships were a fleet under His convoy, and His
great heart went out to them all. Yet He went to sleep,
because He had left in His Father's care even the re-
quests for His love and sympathy. We, who are much
weaker than He, will find strength in doing the same.

The Wisest Choice

Having left everything with His Father, our Lord did
the wisest thing possible. He did just what the hour demanded—He went to sleep! That was the best thing Jesus could do, and sometimes it is the best thing we can
do. Christ was weary and worn, and when anyone is ex-
hausted, it is his duty to go to sleep if he can. The Savior
had to be up again in the morning, preaching and work-
ing miracles, and if He had not slept, He would not
have been fit for His holy duty. Also, it was necessary
for Him to keep Himself in excellent condition for His
service.

Knowing that the time to sleep had come, the Lord
slept, which was the right thing to do. Often, when we
have fretted and worried, we would have glorified God
far more if we had literally gone to sleep. To glorify God
by sleep is not as difficult as some might think. To our
Lord, it was natural.

You may be worried, sad, wearied. The doctor may
have prescribed a medicine for you that does you no
good. But, if you enter into full peace with God and go to
sleep, you will wake up infinitely more refreshed than by
any drug! The sleep that the Lord gives to His beloved
is indeed refreshing and healing. Seek it as Jesus
sought it. Go to bed, brother or sister, and you will better

imitate your Lord than by worrying other people by your mood.

There is also a spiritual sleep in which we ought to imitate Jesus. How often I have worried about my church, until I have come to my senses and have said to myself, "How foolish I am! Can I not depend on God? Is it not much more His cause than mine?" Then I have taken my load in prayer and left it with the Lord. I have said, "In God's name, this matter will never worry me again," and I have left my urgent concern with Him and have ended it forever.

In this way I have deliberately given up many a trying situation into the Lord's care. And when any of my friends have said to me, "What about so and so?" I have simply answered, "I do not know, and I no longer take the trouble to know. The Lord will interpose in some way or other, but I will trouble no more about it."

No horrible turn of events has ever occurred in a matter that I have left in God's care. Keeping my hands out of such things has been pure wisdom. *"Stand still, and see the salvation of the LORD"* (Exod. 14:13) is God's own precept. Let us follow Jesus in this.

Having a child's confidence in the great Father, He retired to the stern of the ship, selected a pillow, deliberately lay down upon it, and went to sleep. Though the ship was filling with water, though it tossed in the waves, He slept on. Nothing could break the peace of His tranquil soul. Every sailor on board reeled to and fro and staggered like a drunken man and was at his wits' end. But Jesus was neither at His wits' end nor did He stagger, for He rested in perfect innocence and undisturbed confidence. His heart was and is happy in God, and therefore He remained peaceful. Oh, for grace to imitate Him!

The Failure of the Disciples

But here notice, dear friends, the difference between the Master and His disciples. While He was in a great calm, they were in a great storm. Observe their failure here. They were just as human as we are, and so we often act just as they did.

Giving Way to Fear

They gave way to fear. They were very much afraid that the ship would sink and that they would all perish. By yielding to fear in this way, they forgot the solid reasons for courage that were close at hand; for, in actuality, they were safe enough. Christ was aboard that vessel, and if the ship were sinking, He would have sunk with them. A heathen sailor took courage during a storm from the fact that Caesar was on board the ship that was tossed by stormy winds. Should not the disciples have felt secure with Jesus on board? Fear not, you carry Jesus and His cause!

Jesus had come to do a work, and His disciples should have known that He could not perish with that work unaccomplished. Could they not trust Him? They had seen Him multiply the loaves and fishes and cast out devils and heal all kinds of sicknesses; could they not trust Him to still the storm? Unreasonable unbelief! Faith in God is true wisdom, but to doubt God is irrational. It is the height of absurdity and folly to question omnipotent love.

Wrongful Accusation

The disciples were also unwise in what they said to the Master. He was extremely weary, and He needed sleep, but they hurried to Him and woke Him in a somewhat rough and irreverent manner. They were slow to do so, but their fear urged them. Therefore, they woke Him, uttering ungenerous and unloving words: *"Master, carest thou not that we perish?"*

Shame on the lips that asked so harsh a question! Did they not greatly blame themselves after thinking about what they had said? Christ had given them no cause for such hard speeches; and, moreover, it was unseemly for them to call Him *"Master"* and then to ask Him, *"Carest thou not that we perish?"* Is He to be accused of such hardheartednesses that He would let His faithful disciples perish when He had power to deliver them? Alas, we, too, have been guilty of similar offenses!

I think I have known some of Christ's disciples who have appeared to doubt the wisdom or the love of their Lord. They did not quite say that He was mistaken, but they said that He moved in a mysterious way. They did not quite complain that He was unkind to them, but they whispered that they could not reconcile His dealings with His infinite love. Alas, Jesus has endured much from our unbelief! May this illustration help us to see our spots, and may the love of our dear Lord remove them!

THE CALM THAT CHRIST CREATED

So far, I have written about the Master's calm and about the disciples' failure. Now let us focus on the great calm that Jesus created. *"There was a great calm."*

By His Voice

His voice produced this calm. It is said that if oil is poured upon water, the water will become smooth. I suppose there is some truth in this statement, but there is all truth in this: if God speaks, the storm subsides into a calm, so that the waves of the sea are still. Our Lord Jesus only has to speak in the heart of any one of us, and immediately *"the peace of God, which passeth all understanding"* (Phil. 4:7) will possess us.

No matter how dreary your despondency, or how dreadful your despair, the Lord can at once create a great calm of confidence. What a door of hope this opens to any who are in trouble! If I could make a poor man rich by speaking to him, if I could make a sick one well by talking to him, I am sure that I would do so at once. But Jesus is infinitely better than I am, and therefore I know that He will speak peace to the tried and troubled heart.

An Immediate Calm

Note, too, that this calm came at once. Jesus *"arose, and rebuked the wind, and said unto the sea, Peace, be still. And the wind ceased, and there was a great calm."* As soon as Jesus spoke, all was quiet. I have met many people who are troubled, and I have seen a few who have slowly come out into light and liberty. But, more frequently, deliverance has come suddenly. The iron gate has opened of its own accord, and the prisoner has stepped into immediate freedom (Acts 12:10–11). *"The snare is broken, and we are escaped"* (Ps. 124:7). What a joy it is to know that rest is so near even when the tempest rages most furiously!

Faith Is Paired with Rest

Note, also, that the Savior coupled this rest with faith, for He said to the disciples as soon as the calm

145

came, *"Why are ye so fearful? how is it that ye have no faith?"* (Mark 4:40). Faith and calm go together. If you believe, you will rest; if you will simply cast yourself upon your God, surrendering absolutely to His will, you will have mercy, joy, and light. Even if we have no faith, the Lord will sometimes give us the blessing that we need, for He delights to do more for us than we have any right to expect of Him. However, usually the rule of His kingdom is, *"According to your faith be it unto you"* (Matt. 9:29).

A Delightful Calm

This great calm is very delightful, and concerning this I want to use my personal testimony. I write from my own knowledge when I say that it *"passeth all understanding"* (Phil. 4:7). The other night I was sitting, meditating on God's mercy and love, when I suddenly found in my own heart a most delightful sense of perfect peace. I had come to Beulah (Isa. 62:4), the land where the sun shines without a cloud. *"There was a great calm."*

I felt as sailors might feel after they have been tossed about in choppy waters, and all of a sudden the ocean becomes as unruffled as a mirror, and the seabirds come and sit in happy circles upon the water. I felt perfectly content, yes, undividedly happy. Not a wave of trouble broke upon the shore of my heart, and even far out to sea in the deeps of my being all was still. I knew no ungratified wish, no unsatisfied desire. I could not discover a reason for uneasiness or a motive for fear. There was nothing close to fanaticism in my feelings, no sign of radical excitement. Rather, my soul was waiting upon God and delighting in Him alone.

Oh, the blessedness of this rest in the Lord! What a paradise it is! This experience was, for me, no different than a fragment of heaven. We often talk about our great spiritual storms. Why should we not speak of our great calms? If ever we get into trouble, how we complain about it! Why should we not sing of our deliverances?

All providence works for our good. Nothing can harm us. The Lord is our shield and our *"exceeding great reward"* (Gen. 15:1). Why, then, should we fear? *"The LORD of hosts is with us; the God of Jacob is our refuge"* (Ps. 46:7). To the believer, peace is no presumption. He is given the full privilege of enjoying *"perfect peace"* (Isa. 26:3)—a quiet that is deep and founded on truth, a calmness that encompasses all things and is not broken by any of the ten thousand disturbing causes that otherwise might prevent our rest. *"Thou wilt keep him in perfect peace, whose mind is stayed on thee: because he trusteth in thee"* (v. 3). Oh, to get into that calm and remain in it until we come to that world where there is no more raging sea!

If we are blessed enough to attain to the calm that ruled within our Savior, it will give us power to make external matters calm. One who has peace can make peace. We cannot work miracles out of our own strength, yet the works that Jesus did we will do also (John 14:12). Sleeping His sleep, we will awake in His renewed energy and treat the winds and waves as things subject to the power of faith, and therefore to be commanded into quiet. We will speak in a way that comforts others: our calm will work marvels in the little ships of which others are captains. We, too, will say, *"Peace, be still."* Our confidence will prove contagious, and the timid will grow brave. Our tender love will spread to others, and the contentious will cool down to patience.

The catch is that the matter must begin within ourselves. We cannot create a calm until we are calm ourselves. It is easier to rule the elements than to govern the unruliness of our own fickle natures. When grace has made us masters of our fears, so that we can take a pillow and fall asleep amid the hurricane, the fury of the tempest is over. He gives peace and safety when He gives sleep to His beloved.

Chapter 12

Real Contact with Jesus

And Jesus said, Somebody hath touched me:
for I perceive that virtue is gone out of me.
—Luke 8:46

Our Lord was very frequently in the midst of a crowd. His preaching was so clear and so forcible that He always attracted a vast number of hearers. Moreover, the rumor of the loaves and fishes no doubt had something to do with increasing His audiences, for the expectation of beholding a miracle would be sure to add to the numbers of the hangers-on. Our Lord Jesus Christ often found it difficult to move through the streets because of the masses who pressed against Him. This was encouraging to Him as a preacher, and yet only a small amount of real good came from all the excitement that gathered around His personal ministry.

Perhaps He looked upon the great mass of people and said, *"What is the chaff to the wheat?"* (Jer. 23:28), for here it was piled upon the threshing-floor, heap upon heap. Yet, after His death, His disciples might have counted only a few converts, for those who had spiritually received Him were but few. Many were called, but few were chosen (Matt. 22:14). Yet, wherever one was blessed, our Savior took note of it; it touched a chord in His soul. He never could be unaware when power had gone out from Him to heal a sick one, or when power had gone forth with His ministry to save a sinful soul.

Of all the crowd that gathered round the Savior on the day of which our text speaks, I find nothing said about one of them except this solitary *"somebody"* who had touched Him. The crowd came and the crowd went, but little is recorded of it all. Just as the ocean leaves very little behind it when it has reached full tide and recedes again to deeper waters, so the vast multitude around the Savior left only this one precious deposit— one *"somebody"* who had touched Him and had received miraculous power from Him.

On Sunday mornings, the crowds come pouring into the churches like a mighty ocean, and then they all withdraw again. Here and there a *"somebody"* is left weeping for sin, a *"somebody"* is left rejoicing in Christ, a *"somebody"* is left who can say, "I have touched the hem of His garment, and I have been made whole." (See Matthew 9:21.) May God find these few people when they reach out for Him, and all the praise will be His!

Jesus said, *"Somebody hath touched me."* From this, we observe that we should never be satisfied unless we get into personal contact with Christ, so that we touch Him as this woman touched His garment. Secondly, if we can get into such personal contact, we will have a blessing: *"I perceive that virtue is gone out of me."* Thirdly, if we do get a blessing, Christ will know it. However obscure our case may be, He will know it, and He will have us make it known to others. He will speak and ask the questions that will draw us out and manifest us to the world.

OUR MAIN GOAL: PERSONAL CONTACT WITH CHRIST

First, then, let it be our chief aim and objective to come into personal contact with the Lord Jesus Christ. Peter said, *"The multitude throng thee and press thee"* (Luke 8:45), and that is true of the multitude to this very day. But of those who come where Christ is in the assembly of His people, a large proportion only come because it is their custom to do so.

Perhaps such people hardly know why they go to a place of worship. They go because they have always gone, and they think it is wrong not to go. They are just like doors that swing upon their hinges; they take no interest in what is going on, and they do not and cannot enter into the heart and soul of the service. They are glad if the sermon is rather short, for then there is less boredom for them. They are glad if they can look around and gaze at the congregation, for then there is something to interest them. But getting near to the Lord Jesus is not what they hope to find. They have not looked at it in that light.

They come and they go, and they will keep coming and going, until eventually they will come for the last time and they will find out in the next world that the means of grace were not instituted to be matters of custom. They will suddenly discover that to have heard Jesus Christ preached, and to have rejected Him, is no trifle, but a solemn thing for which they will have to answer in the presence of the great Judge of all the earth.

There are others who come to the house of prayer and try to enter into the service, and do so in a self-righteous fashion. They may come to the Lord's Table. They may even join the church. They are baptized, yet

151

not by the Holy Spirit. They take Communion, but they do not take the Lord Himself; they eat the bread, but they never eat His flesh; they drink the wine, but they never drink His blood. They have been immersed in water, but they have never been buried with Christ in baptism, nor have they risen again with Him into newness of life. To them, reading, singing, kneeling, hearing, and so on, are enough. They are content with the shell, but they know nothing of the blessed spiritual kernel, the true *"marrow and fatness"* (Ps. 63:5).

These are the majority, no matter what church you may choose. They press in around Jesus, but they do not touch Him. They come, but they do not come into contact with Jesus. They are outward, external hearers only, but there is no inward touching of the blessed person of Christ, no spiritual contact with the ever blessed Savior, no stream of life and love flowing from Him to them. It is all mechanical religion. They know nothing of vital godliness.

But, *"Somebody,"* said Christ, *"hath touched me,"* and that is the soul of the matter. Dear reader, when you are alone in prayer, never be satisfied with having prayed. Do not give up until you have touched Christ in prayer. If you have not reached Him, sigh and cry until you do! Do not think you have already prayed, but try again. Also, when you go to church, do not be satisfied with listening to the sermon, and so on. Do not be content unless you gain access to Christ the Master and touch Him.

When you come to the Communion table, do not consider it an ordinance of grace to you unless you have gone right through the veil (Heb. 6:19–20) and into Christ's own arms, or at least have touched His garment. The life and soul of Communion is to touch Jesus Christ

Himself, and unless *"somebody"* has touched Him, the ceremony is just a dead performance, without life or power.

The woman in our text verse was not only among those who were in the crowd, but she also touched Jesus. Therefore, dear readers, let me hold her up as our example in some respects, though in other respects I pray that you might excel her.

Under Many Difficulties

First, she felt that it was of no use being in the crowd or being on the same street with Christ, or near to the place where He was, unless she could get at Him. She knew she had to touch Him. You will notice that she did so under many difficulties. There was a great crowd. She was a woman. She was also a woman weakened by a long-term disease that had drained her strength and had left her more fit for lying in bed than for struggling in the seething tumult. Yet, notwithstanding that, her desire was so intense that she pressed on, probably enduring many shoves and bruises. At last, this poor trembling woman got near to the Lord.

Beloved, it is not always easy to get at Jesus. It is very easy to kneel down to pray, but not so easy to reach Christ in prayer. Perhaps the cries of your own child have often hindered you when you were striving to approach Jesus. Perhaps a knock comes at the door when you most wish to be alone. When you are sitting in the house of God, the person seated in front of you may unconsciously distract your attention. It is not easy to draw near to Christ, especially when you come directly from your workplace with a thousand thoughts and cares about you. You cannot always unload your burden outside and go into the sanctuary with your heart prepared to receive the Gospel.

Ah, it is a terrible fight sometimes, a real fight with evil, with temptation, and I do not know what else. But, beloved, do fight it out! Do not let your times of prayer be wasted or your opportunities for hearing be thrown away, but, like this woman, be resolved that, in all your weakness, you will lay hold of Christ. And then, if you are resolved about it and you still cannot get to Him, He will come to you. When you are struggling against unbelieving thoughts, He will turn and say, "Make room for that poor feeble one, so that she may come to Me, for My desire is toward the work of My own hands. Let her come to Me, and let her desire be granted to her."

In Secret

Observe, also, that this woman touched Jesus very secretly. Perhaps you are getting near to Christ at this very moment, and yet you have gained so little contact with Christ that the joyous flush and the sparkle in the eye, which we often see in the child of God, have not yet come to you. But, though your touch is in secret, it is true. Although you cannot yet tell another about it, it is accomplished. You have touched Jesus.

Beloved, it is not always the closest fellowship with Christ of which we talk the most. Deep waters are still and calm. I suppose that we sometimes get nearer to Christ when we think we are at a distance than we do when we imagine we are near Him, for we are not always exactly the best judges of our own spiritual states. We may be very close to the Master, and yet we may be so anxious to get closer that we feel dissatisfied with the measure of grace that we have already received. To be satisfied with self is not a sign of grace, but to long for more grace is often a far better evidence of the healthy state of the soul.

Friend, go to the Master in secret. If you do not dare to tell your wife or your child or your father that you are trusting in Jesus, it need not be told as yet. You may do it secretly, as the believer did to whom Jesus said, *"When thou wast under the fig tree, I saw thee"* (John 1:48). Nathanael had retired to the shade so that no one might see him, but Jesus saw him and took note of his prayer. Likewise, Jesus will see you in the crowd or in the dark, and He will not withhold His blessing.

Under a Sense of Unworthiness

This woman also came into contact with Christ under a very deep sense of unworthiness. I imagine she thought, "If I touch the Great Prophet, it will be remarkable if He does not strike me down with some sudden judgment," for her sickness had designated her as an unclean woman. She had no right to be in the crowd. If the Levitical law had been strictly carried out, I suppose she would have been confined to her house. But she was wandering about, and she needed to go and touch the holy Savior.

Ah, poor heart, you feel that you are not fit to touch the hem of the Master's robe, for you are so unworthy. You have never felt so undeserving as you do now. When you think back on last week and its struggles, when you think of the present state of your heart and all its wanderings from God, you feel as if there never was a sinner as worthless as you. "Is grace for me?" you ask. "Is Christ for me?" Oh, yes, unworthy one, He is! Do not go away without touching Him.

Jesus Christ does not save the worthy, but the unworthy. Your plea must not be righteousness, but guilt. And, though you are ashamed of yourself, Jesus is not ashamed of you, for you are a child of God. Though you feel unfit to come, let your unfitness only urge you on with a greater earnestness of desire. Let your sense of need make you more fervent to approach the Lord, who can supply your need.

Thus, you see, the woman came under difficulties, she came secretly, she came as an unworthy one, but still she obtained the blessing.

Trembling in Faith

This woman touched the Master very tremblingly, and it was only a hurried touch, but still it was the touch of faith. Oh, to lay hold of Christ! Be thankful if you get near Him even for a few minutes. "Abide with me," should be your prayer; but oh, if He only gives you a glimpse of Himself, be thankful! Remember that a single touch healed the woman. She did not embrace Christ for hours. She had only a touch, and she was healed.

Beloved, may you catch a glimpse of Jesus now! Though it is only a glimpse, it will delight and comfort your soul. Perhaps you are waiting for Christ, desiring His company, and while you are turning this over in your mind you are asking, "Will He ever shine upon me? Will He ever speak loving words to me? Will He ever let me sit at His feet? Will He ever permit me to rest my head in His lap?" Come and try Him. Though you may shake like a leaf, come.

Sometimes they come best who come most tremblingly, for when the creature is lowest, then the Creator is highest; and when in our own esteem we are less than nothing, then Christ is fairer and lovelier in our eyes. One of the best ways to reach heaven is on our hands and knees. At any rate, there is no fear of falling when we are in that position.

Let your lowliness of heart, your sense of utter nothingness, be a sweet means of leading you to receive more of Christ, instead of disqualifying you. The emptier I am, the more room there is for my Master. The more I lack, the more He will give me. The more I feel my sickness, the more I will adore and bless Him when He makes me whole.

You see, the woman really did touch Christ, and so I come back to that. Whatever infirmity there was in the touch, it was a real touch of faith. She did reach Christ Himself. She did not touch Peter; that would have been of no use to her. She did not touch John or James; that would have been no good to her. She touched the Master Himself.

Do not be content unless you can do the same. Put out the hand of faith, and touch Christ. Rest on Him. Rely on His bloody sacrifice, His dying love, His rising power, His ascended plea. As you rest in Him, your vital touch, however feeble, will certainly give you the blessing your soul needs.

This leads me to say what the results of this touch were.

The Result: Healing and Wholeness

The woman in the crowd did touch Jesus, and having done so, she received power from Him. The healing energy streamed at once through the finger of faith into the woman. In Christ there is healing for all spiritual diseases. There is a speedy healing, a healing that will not take months or years but that is complete in one second.

In Christ there is a sufficient healing, though your diseases might be multiplied beyond all comparison. In Christ there is an all-conquering power to drive out every illness. Though, like this woman, you baffle physicians and your case is considered desperate beyond all others, a touch from Christ will heal you.

What a precious, glorious Gospel we have to preach to sinners! If they touch Jesus when the Devil himself is in them, that touch of faith will drive the Devil out. Even though you may have been like the man into whom a legion of devils had entered, the word of Jesus cast them all into the deep, and you sat at His feet, clothed and in your right mind. (See Mark 5:1–15.) There is no excess or extravagance of sin that the power of Jesus Christ cannot overcome.

If you can believe, you will be saved, no matter what you have been in the past. If you can believe, even though you have been lying in scarlet dye until your whole being has been stained red by sin, the precious blood of Jesus will make you white as snow. Though you have become black as hell itself and only fit to be cast into the pit, if you trust Jesus, your simple faith will give to your soul the healing that will make you fit to walk the streets of heaven and to stand before Jehovah-Rophi's face, magnifying *"the LORD that healeth thee"* (Exod. 15:26).

And now, child of God, I want you to learn the same lesson. You may have said of yourself, "Alas, I feel very dull; my spirituality is at a very low ebb. The spirit is willing, but the flesh is weak. Most likely I will have no holy joy today!" Why not? The touch of Jesus could make you live if you were dead, and surely it will stir the little

life that is in you, though it may seem to you that it is
dying!

Struggle hard, my friend, to get at Jesus! May the
eternal Spirit come and help you, and may you yet find
that your dull, dead times can soon become your best
times. Oh, what a blessing it is that God *"lifteth up the
beggar from the dunghill"* (1 Sam. 2:8)! He does not raise
us when He sees that we are already up. Instead, when
He finds us lying low, then He delights to lift us up and
set us among princes (v. 8). In a single moment, you may
mount up from the depths of heaviness to the very
heights of ecstatic worship, if you can only touch Christ
crucified. View Him there, with streaming wounds, with
thorn-crowned head, as He dies for you in all the majesty
of His misery!

But then, you say, "I have a thousand doubts right
now." Ah, but your doubts will soon vanish when you
draw near to Christ. Anyone who feels the touch of
Christ never doubts, at least not while the touch lasts,
for observe this woman! She felt in her body that she was
made whole, and so will you, if you will only come into
contact with the Lord. Do not wait for proof, but come to
Christ for proof. If you cannot even dream of a good
thing in yourself, come to Jesus Christ as you did at the
first. Come as if you never had come at all. Come to Jesus as a sinner, and your doubts will flee away.

Another complains, "But I know about all the sins I
have committed since my conversion." Well, return to
Jesus when your guilt seems to return. The fountain is
still open, and that fountain, you will remember, is open
not only for sinners, but also for saints. The Scriptures
say, *"There shall be a fountain opened to the house of
David and to the inhabitants of Jerusalem"* (Zech. 13:1).
That is, there is a fountain for you, for believers in Jesus.

The fountain is still open. Come to Jesus anew, and whatever your sins or doubts or burdens may be, they will all depart as soon as you can touch your Lord.

HE KNOWS WHEN YOU TOUCH HIM

My next observation is, if somebody touches Jesus, the Lord will know it. You may be a stranger to many people, but that does not matter. Your name is *"Somebody,"* and Christ will know you. If you get a blessing, there will be two who will know it—you and Christ. Oh, if you will look to Jesus today, it might not be known to others, and your neighbors might not hear of it, but still it will be registered in the courts of heaven. All the bells of the New Jerusalem will ring, and all the angels will rejoice (Luke 15:10) as soon as they know that you are born again.

"Somebody!" I do not know your name, but— *"Somebody!"*—God's electing love rests on you; Christ's redeeming blood was shed for you; and the Spirit has brought about a work in you, or you would not have touched Jesus. Jesus knows all of this.

It is a consoling thought that Christ not only knows the prominent children in the family, but He also knows the little ones. This stands fast: *"The Lord knoweth them that are his"* (2 Tim. 2:19), whether they have just come to know Him now, or whether they have known Him for fifty years. *"The Lord knoweth them that are his."* If I am a part of Christ's body, I may be just the foot, but the Lord knows the foot. The head and the heart in heaven feel when the foot on earth is bruised.

If you have touched Jesus, I tell you that amid the glories of angels and the everlasting hallelujahs of all the blood-bought believers, He has found time to hear your sigh, to receive your faith, and to give you an answer of peace. All the way from heaven to earth there has rushed a mighty stream of healing power, which has come from Christ to you. Since you have touched Him, the healing power has touched you.

MAKE IT KNOWN TO OTHERS

Now, since Jesus knows of your salvation, He wishes other people to know of it, too. That is why He has put it into my heart to say, "Somebody has touched the Lord." Where is that somebody? Somebody, where are you? You have touched Christ, though with a weak finger, and you are now saved. Make it known to your fellow Christians. It is due them to let them know. You cannot guess what joy it gives other believers when they hear of sick ones being healed by the Master.

Perhaps you have known the Lord for months and you have not yet made an open acknowledgment of it. Do not hold back any longer, but go forth tremblingly, as this woman did. Perhaps you may say, "I do not know what to say." Well, you must tell what this woman told the Lord; she told Him the whole truth. Your fellow believers do not want anything else. They do not desire any sham experience. They do not want you to manufacture feelings like somebody else's that you have read of in a book. Go and tell what you have felt. No one will ask you to tell what you have not felt or what you do not know. But, if you have touched Christ and you have been healed, go and tell your brothers and sisters in Christ what the Lord has done for your soul.

And, when you draw near to Christ and have a sweet season of communion with Him, tell it to your fellow believers. After hearing a sermon, take home spiritual food for those in your family who could not attend church that day. God grant that you may always have something sweet to tell about what you have known of precious truth.

Whoever you may be, though you may be nothing but a poor *"somebody,"* if you have touched Christ, tell others about it. In this way, they may come and touch Him, too.

Chapter 13

A Word from the
Beloved's Mouth

He that is washed needeth not save to
wash his feet, but is clean every whit:
and ye are clean.
—John 13:10

Gideon's fleece was so full of dew that he could wring out the moisture. In the same manner, sometimes a verse of Scripture will be very full of meaning when the Holy Spirit visits His servants through its words. This statement of our Savior to His disciples has been to me like bread dipped in honey, and I do not doubt that it will prove equally as sweet to you, as well.

THE ANCIENT BLESSING

Observe carefully, dear reader, the high praise that is given to the Lord's beloved disciples: *"Ye are clean."* This is the ancient blessing, lost so quickly by our first parents. The loss of this virtue shut man out of Paradise and continues to shut men out of heaven. The lack of cleanness in their hearts and upon their hands condemns sinners to banishment from God and defiles all their offerings. To be clean before God is the desire of every repentant person, and it is the highest aspiration of the most advanced believer. It is what all the ceremonies and cleansings of the law can never bestow and what Pharisees, with all their pretensions, cannot attain. To be clean is to be like the angels, like glorified saints, even like the Father Himself.

Acceptance with the Lord, safety, happiness, and every blessing, always accompany cleanness of heart. The one who has a clean heart cannot miss out on heaven. A clean heart seems too high a condition to be ascribed to mortals, yet, by the lips of Him who could not err, the disciples were said to be *"clean."* There was no qualifying phrase, no condition for their cleanness. They were perfectly justified in the sight of eternal equity and were regarded as free from every impurity.

Is this blessing yours? Have you ever believed so that you might receive Christ's righteousness? Have you taken the Lord Jesus to be your complete cleansing, your sanctification, your redemption? Has the Holy Spirit ever sealed in your peaceful spirit the gracious testimony, *"Ye are clean"*? The assurance is not confined to the apostles, for you also are *"complete in him"* (Col. 2:10) and *"perfect in Christ Jesus"* (Col. 1:28), if you have indeed by faith received the righteousness of God.

The psalmist said, *"Wash me, and I shall be whiter than snow"* (Ps. 51:7). If you have been washed, you are clean before the Lord to the highest and purest degree, and you are clean now. Oh, that all believers would live up to this privilege! But, unfortunately, too many are as depressed as if they were still miserable sinners, and they forget that they are forgiven in Christ Jesus and therefore ought to be happy in the Lord. Remember, beloved believer, because you are one with Christ, you are not with sinners *"in the gall of bitterness"* (Acts 8:23) but with the saints in the *"land that floweth with milk and honey"* (Num. 16:13).

Your cleanness is not measured by any scale or ruler; it is not a variable or vanishing quantity. Instead, it is present, constant, and perfect. You are clean through the Word, through the application of *"the blood of sprinkling"* (Heb. 12:24) to your conscience, and through the imputation of the righteousness of the Lord Jesus Christ.

Lift up your head, therefore, and sing with a joyful heart, because your transgression has been pardoned, your sin has been covered, and Jehovah sees no iniquity in you. Do not let another moment pass until by faith in Jesus you have grasped this privilege. Do not be content to merely believe that the priceless gift may be had, but lay hold of it for yourself. You will find that the song praising Christ's substitutionary death for you is an excellent song, if you are able to sing it.

THE ONE WHO GIVES THE PRAISE

Much of the force of our text, *"And ye are clean,"* lies in the One giving the praise. To receive the approval of our fellowmen is consoling, but in the end it is of small consequence. The human standard of purity is itself grossly incorrect, and therefore to be judged by it is a poor test, and to be acquitted by it is a slender comfort. However, the Lord Jesus judges no one according to the flesh. He came forth from God and is Himself God, infinitely just and good. Hence, His tests are accurate, and His verdict is absolute.

I have come to know that whomever He pronounces clean is clean indeed. Our Lord is omniscient, so He can at once detect the least evil in His disciples. If unpardoned sin remains with an individual, He has to have seen it. If any former condemnation were lingering upon someone, He would detect it at once, for no speck could escape His all-discerning eye. Even so, He said without hesitation to all the disciples but Judas, *"Ye are clean."*

Perhaps they did not catch the full glory of this pronouncement. They might have missed much of the deep, joyous meaning that is now revealed to us by the Spirit. Otherwise, what bliss to have heard with their own ears from those sacred lips so plain, so positive, so sure a testimony of their character before God! Yet our hearts do not need to be filled with regret because we cannot hear that ever blessed voice with our earthly ears, for the testimony of Jesus in the Word is quite as sure as the witness of His lips when He spoke among the sons of men. And that testimony is, *"All that believe are justified from all things"* (Acts 13:39).

Yes, this promise is as certain as if you heard the Redeemer Himself say it. You are free from all condemning sin if you are looking with your whole heart to Jesus as your all in all. What a joy is yours and mine! He who is to judge the world in righteousness has Himself confirmed that we are clean. However black and terrible the condemnation of guilt is, the forgiveness of our sins is that much brighter and more comforting. Let us rejoice in the Lord, whose indisputable judgment has given forth a blessing so joyous, so full of glory.

> Jesus declares me clean,
> Then clean indeed I am,
> However guilty I have been,
> I'm cleansèd through the Lamb.

THOSE WHO ARE PRAISED

It may encourage you to call to mind the people who were praised. They were not cherubim and seraphim, but men, and notably they were men filled with weakness. There was Peter, who a few minutes afterward was brash and presumptuous. But it is not necessary to name them one by one, for they all forsook their Master and fled in His hour of peril. Not one among them was more than a mere child in grace. They had little about them that was apostolic except their commission. They were very evidently men who had the same passions that we do, yet their Lord declared them to be clean, and clean they were.

This is nourishment for those souls who are hungering for righteousness and worrying because they feel so much of the burden of indwelling sin: cleanliness before the Lord is not destroyed by our sins and weaknesses or prevented by our inward temptations. We stand in the righteousness of Another. No amount of personal weakness, spiritual anxiety, soul conflict, or mental agony can mar our acceptance in the Beloved. We may be weak infants or wandering sheep, and for both reasons we may be very far from what we wish to be. But, as God sees us, we are viewed as washed in the blood of Jesus, and we, even we, are *"clean every whit."*

What a forcible expression, *"clean every whit"*— every inch, from every point of view, in all respects, and to the uttermost degree! Dear friend, if you are a believer, this fact is true even for you. Do not hesitate to drink of it, for it is water out of your own well, given to you in the covenant of grace. Do not think that it is presumptuous to believe this statement, as marvelous as it is. You are dealing with a wonderful Savior, who only does wonderful things. Therefore, do not stand back on account of the greatness of the blessing, but rather believe even more readily because the message is so similar to everything the Lord says or does.

Yet, when you have believed for yourself and have cast every doubt to the wind, you will not wonder less, but more. Your never ceasing cry will then be, *"Whence is this to me?"* (Luke 1:43). How is it that I, who wallowed with swine, should be made as pure as the angels? Since I have been delivered from the foulest guilt, is it indeed possible that I am now the possessor of a perfect righteousness? Sing, O heavens, for the Lord has done it, and He shall have everlasting praise!

When the Praise Was Given

The time when the praise was given is also a lesson to us. The word of loving judgment is in the present tense: *"Ye are clean."* It is not, "Ye were clean," which might be a condemnation for willful neglect, a prophecy of wrath to come, or a rebuke for purity that has been shamelessly defiled. Nor is it, "Ye might have been clean," which would have been a stern rebuke for privileges rejected and opportunities wasted. Nor is it even, "Ye shall be clean," though that would have been a delightful prophecy of good things to come at some distant time. But it is, *"ye are clean,"* at this moment, wherever you are sitting. Even Peter, who had just spoken so rudely, was then clean.

This is a great comfort amid our present sense of imperfection! Our cleanness is a matter of this present hour. We are, in our present condition and position, *"clean every whit."* Why then postpone our joy? The reason for it is in our possession, so let our joy overflow even now.

Much of our heritage is certainly to come in the future, but if no other blessing were tangible to our faith in this immediate present, this one blessing alone should awaken all our powers to the highest praise. Even now we are clothed with the fair white linen that is the righteousness of believers, for we are washed in the blood of Christ and pardoned by His name. May the Holy Spirit bear witness with every believer that *"ye are clean."*

Chapter 14

Comfort
and Consolation

I will not leave you comfortless:
I will come to you.
—John 14:18

If we use the translation of this verse that is provided in the margin of the King James Version, the verse reads, *"I will not leave you orphans: I will come to you."* In the absence of our Lord Jesus Christ, the disciples were like children deprived of their parents. During the three years in which He had been with them, He had solved all their difficulties, borne all their burdens, and supplied all their needs. Whenever a case was too hard or too heavy for them, they took it to Him. When their enemies nearly overcame them, Jesus came to the rescue and turned the tide of battle.

They were all happy and safe enough while the Master was with them; He walked in their midst like a father amid a large family of children, making the whole household glad. But He was about to be taken from them by a shameful death, and they probably felt that they

171

would be like little children deprived of their natural and beloved protector. Our Savior knew the fear that was in their hearts, and before they could express it, He removed it by saying, "You will not be left alone in this wild and barren world; though I may be absent in the flesh, I will be present with you in a more effective way. I will come to you spiritually, and you will derive from My spiritual presence even more good than you could have had from My bodily presence, had I still continued in your midst."

Observe, first, that an evil is averted here: *"I will not leave you orphans."* In the second place, a consolation is provided: *"I will come to you."*

An Evil Averted

Without their Lord, and apart from the Holy Spirit, believers would be like other orphans, unhappy and desolate. Give them what you may, their loss cannot be recompensed. No number of lamps can make up for the sun's absence; shine as they may, it is still night. No circle of friends can compensate for the loss of a woman's husband; without him, she is still a widow. Without Jesus, it is inevitable that believers should be like orphans, but Jesus has promised that we will not be so. He declares that we will have the one thing that can remove the desolation: *"I will come to you."*

What Makes One an Orphan

Now remember, an orphan is someone whose parents are dead. This in itself is a great sorrow, for the father can no longer love his children and protect them and provide for them as he once did. But we are not orphans in that sense, for our Lord Jesus is not dead. It is true that He died, for one of the soldiers pierced His side with a spear, and blood and water came out from the wound. This was certain proof that the fountain of life had been broken up. He died, certainly, but He is not dead now. Do not go to the grave to seek Him. Angel voices say, *"He is not here: for he is risen"* (Matt. 28:6). He could not be held captive by the bonds of death.

We do not worship a dead Christ, nor do we even think of Him now as a corpse. Oh, it is so good to think of Christ as living, remaining in a real and true existence. He is no less alive because He died, but all the more truly full of life because He has passed through the gates of the grave and is now reigning forever. See, then, the bitter root of the orphan's sorrow is gone from us, for our Jesus is not dead now. No mausoleum enshrines His ashes, no pyramid entombs His body, no monument records the place of His permanent sepulchre.

> He lives, the great Redeemer lives,
> What joy the blest assurance gives!

We are not orphans, for *"the Lord is risen indeed"* (Luke 24:34).

Not Left Alone

One of the greatest sorrows that an orphan has springing out of the death of his parent is that he is left alone. He cannot now make appeals to the wisdom of the parent who could direct him. He cannot run, when he is weary, to climb on his father's knee as he once did. He cannot lean his aching head against his parent's chest. "Father," he may say, but no voice answers him. "Mother," he may cry, but that fond title, which would awaken the mother if she slept, cannot arouse her from the bed of death. The child is alone, far from those two hearts which were his best companions. The parents are gone. Such little ones know what it is to be deserted and forsaken.

But we are not so; we are not orphans. It is true that Jesus is not here in body, but His spiritual presence is quite as blessed as His bodily presence would have been. Actually, it is better, for if Jesus Christ were here in person, we could not all come and touch the hem of His garment—not all at once, at any rate. There might be thousands waiting all over the world to speak with Him, but how could they all reach Him if He were merely here in body? Everyone might be waiting to tell Him something, but in the body He could only receive one or two at a time.

But there is no need for you to say a word; Jesus hears your thoughts and attends to all your needs in the same moment. There is no need to press to get at Him because the crowd is large, for He is as near to me as He is to you, and as near to you as to believers all over the world. He is present everywhere, and all His beloved may talk with Him. You can tell Him at this moment the sorrows that you dare not open up to anyone else. In declaring them to Him, you will feel that you have hardly breathed them into the air before He has heard you. He is a real person, one so real that it is as if you could grip His hand and see the loving sparkle of His eye and the sympathetic look of His countenance.

Is it not this way with you? You know that you have *"a friend that sticketh closer than a brother"* (Prov. 18:24). You have a near and dear One. You are not an orphan; the *"Wonderful, Counsellor, The mighty God, The everlasting Father, The Prince of Peace"* (Isa. 9:6) is with you. Your Lord is here, and He comforts you, as a mother comforts her child.

Not without Provisions

The orphan, too, has lost the hands that always took care to provide food, clothing, and a comfortable home. Poor feeble one, who will provide for his needs? His parents are gone; who will take care of the little wanderer now?

But it is not so with us. Jesus has not left us as orphans. His care for His people is no less now than it was when He sat at the table with Mary, Martha, and Lazarus. Instead of the provisions being less, they are even greater. For, since the Holy Spirit has been given to us, we have richer fare and are more indulged with spiritual comforts than believers were before the Master's bodily form departed. Is your soul hungry? Jesus gives you the bread of heaven. Is your soul thirsty? The waters from the rock do not cease to flow.

Come to Jesus, and make your needs, your burdens, known to Him. You only have to make your needs known to have them all supplied. Christ waits to be gracious to you. He stands with His golden hand open to supply the needs of every living soul. "Oh," says one, "*I am poor and needy.*'" Then go on with the quotation: *"Yet the Lord thinketh upon me"* (Ps. 40:17). "Ah," says another, "I have asked the Lord three times to take away a thorn in the flesh from me." Remember what He said to Paul: *"My grace is sufficient for thee"* (2 Cor. 12:9). You are not left without the strength you need.

The Lord is still your Shepherd. He will provide for you until He leads you through death's dark valley and brings you to the shining pastures upon the hilltops of glory. You are not destitute; you do not need to compromise with this world by bowing to its demands or trusting its vain promises, for Jesus will never leave you or forsake you (Heb. 13:5).

Not without Suitable Instruction

The orphan, too, is left without the instruction that is most suitable for a child. We may say what we will, but there is no one as fit to form a child's character as the parent. It is a very sad loss for a child to have lost either father or mother, for the most skillful teacher, though he may do much, can hardly make up for the way a parent's love can mold a child's mind.

But, dear friends, we are not orphans; we who believe in Jesus are not left without an education. Jesus is not here Himself, it is true. I imagine some of you wish you could go to church on Sundays and listen to Him! Would it not be wonderful to look up at the pulpit and see the Crucified One, and to hear Him preach? Ah, so you think, but the apostle said, *"Though we have known Christ after the flesh, yet now henceforth know we him no more"* (2 Cor. 5:16).

It is profitable that you should receive the Spirit of truth, not through the golden vessel of Christ in His actual presence, but through the poor earthen vessels of humble servants of God. At any rate, whether a preacher speaks or an angel from heaven speaks, the speaker does not matter; it is the Spirit of God alone who is the power of the Word and who makes that Word vital and life-giving for you.

Now, you have the Spirit of God. The Holy Spirit is given so that you may understand every truth of the Scriptures. You may be led into the deepest mysteries by

His teaching. You may be enabled to know and to comprehend those things in the Word of God that have puzzled you for a long time. When you humbly look up to Jesus, His Spirit will still teach you. Even if you could scarcely read a word of the Bible, you would be better instructed than doctors of divinity if you went to the Holy Spirit and were taught by Him in the things of God. Those who go only to books and to the letter of the law, and who are taught by men, are fools in the sight of God; but those who go to Jesus and sit at His feet and ask to be taught by His Spirit, will be *"wise unto salvation"* (2 Tim. 3:15). Blessed be God, we are not left as orphans; we have an Instructor with us still.

Not Lacking a Defender

There is one point in which the orphan is often sorrowfully reminded of his orphanhood, namely, in lacking a defender. It is so natural in little children, when some big bully harasses them, to say, "I'll tell my father!" How often we hear little ones say, "I'll tell Mother!" Sometimes, not being able to do this is a much greater loss than we can guess. Cruel thieves might come and snatch away from orphans the little that a father's love had left behind, and in the court of law there has been no defender to protect the orphan's possessions. Had the father been there, the child would have had his rights; but, in the absence of the father, the orphan is eaten up like bread, and the wicked of the earth devour his possessions.

In this sense, believers are not orphans. The Devil would rob us of our heritage if he could, but there is an Advocate with the Father who pleads for us. Satan would snatch from us every promise and tear from us all the comforts of the covenant, but we are not orphans. When the Enemy brings a suit against us and thinks that we are the only defendants in the case, he is mistaken, for we have an Advocate on high. Christ comes in and pleads, as the sinners' Friend, for us; and when He pleads at the bar of justice, there is no fear that His plea will be ineffective or that our inheritance is not safe. He has not left us orphans.

You who love the Master, you are not alone in this world. Even if you have no earthly friends, if you have no one to whom you can take your cares, if you are quite lonely, Jesus is with you, is really with you, practically with you, able to help you, and ready to do so. You have a good and kind Protector close at hand at this present moment, for Christ has said it: *"I will not leave you orphans."*

CONSOLATION PROVIDED

The second comment I wish to make about our text is that it provides consolation for us. Not only are we saved from being without our Father, but the Lord Jesus also said, *"I will come to you."*

Jesus Comes to Us by the Spirit

What does this mean? From the context, we may suppose that it means, *"'I will come to you'* by My Spirit." Beloved, we must not confuse the persons of the Godhead. The Holy Spirit is not the Son of God; Jesus, the Son of God, is not the Holy Spirit. They are two distinct persons of the one Godhead. But there is such a wonderful unity, and the blessed Spirit acts so marvelously as the Agent of Christ, that it is quite correct to say that, when the Spirit comes, Jesus comes, too. Thus, *"I will come to you"* means, "I, by My Spirit, who will take My place and represent Me, will come to be with you."

See then, Christian, you have the Holy Spirit in you and with you to be the Representative of Christ. Christ is with you now, not in person, but by His Representative—an efficient, almighty, divine, everlasting Representative, who stands for Christ and is like Christ in your soul. Because you have Christ by His Spirit in this way, you cannot be an orphan, for the Spirit of God is always with you.

It is a delightful truth that the Spirit of God always dwells in believers—not sometimes, but always. He is not always active in believers, and He may be grieved until His perceptible presence is altogether withdrawn, but His secret presence is always there. At no single moment is the Spirit of God wholly gone from a believer. The believer would die spiritually if this could happen, but that cannot be, for Jesus has said, *"Because I live, ye shall live also"* (John 14:19).

Even when the believer sins, the Holy Spirit does not utterly depart from him, but He is still in him to make him regret the sin into which he has fallen. The believer's prayers prove that the Holy Spirit is still within him. *"Take not thy holy spirit from me"* (Ps. 51:11) was the prayer of a believer who had fallen very far but with whom the Spirit of God still resided, notwithstanding all the foulness of his guilt and sin.

Visits from the Spirit

In addition to this, Jesus Christ by His Spirit makes certain kinds of visits to His people. The Holy Spirit becomes wonderfully active and powerful at certain times of refreshment. We are then especially and joyfully aware of His divine power. His influence streams through every part of our natures and floods our dark souls with His glorious rays, as the sun shining at midday. Oh, how delightful this is! Sometimes we have felt this at the Communion table. I am equally sure that Jesus Christ has come to us at prayer meetings, during the preaching of the Word, in private meditation, and in searching the Scriptures.

Let us ask the Lord to permit us once again to feel the truth of the promise, *"I will not leave you orphans: I will come to you."*

All His Words Are Instructive

And now, let me remind you that every word of our text verse is instructive: *"I will not leave you orphans: I will come to you."* Observe that the *"I"* is there twice. We can hear Jesus saying, *"'I will not leave you orphans.'* Your fathers and mothers may, but I will not. Friends who once loved you may become hardhearted, but I will not. Judas may play the traitor, and Ahithophel may betray his David, but *'I will not leave you comfortless.'* You have had many disappointments, great heartbreaking sorrows, but I have never caused you any. I, the faithful and true Witness, the immutable, the unchangeable Jesus, the same yesterday, today, and forever—*'I will not leave you comfortless: I will come to you.'"*

Grasp onto that word, *"I,"* and let your soul say, *"'Lord, I am not worthy that thou shouldest come under my roof'* (Matt. 8:8). If You had said, 'I will send an angel to you,' it would have been a great mercy, but You say, *'I will come to you.'* If You had asked some of my fellow Christians to come and speak a word of comfort to me, I would have been thankful, but You have put it in the first person: *'I will come to you.'* O my Lord, what shall I say, what shall I do, but feel a hungering and a thirsting for You, which nothing can satisfy until You fulfill Your own word: *'I will not leave you comfortless: I will come to you'?"*

And then notice the people to whom it was addressed: *"'I will not leave you comfortless.'* You, Peter, who will deny Me; you, Thomas, who will doubt Me—*'I will not leave you comfortless.'"* You who are so insignificant in Israel that you sometimes think that you are so worthless, so unworthy, He will not leave you comfortless, not even you! "O Lord," you say, "if You would look after the rest of Your sheep, I would bless You for Your tenderness to them, but I—I deserve to be left. If I were forsaken by You, I could not blame You, for I have played the harlot against Your love. Yet You continue to say to me, *'I will not leave you.'"*

Heir of heaven, do not lose your part in this promise. Say to Him, "Lord, come unto me, and though You refresh all my fellowmen, refresh me with some of the drops of Your love. O Lord, fill the cup for me; my thirsty spirit pants for it. Fulfill Your word to me, as I stand like Hannah in Your presence. Come unto me, Your servant, unworthy to lift so much as my eyes toward heaven and only daring to say, *'God be merciful to me a sinner'* (Luke 18:13). Fulfill Your promise even to me, *'I will not leave you comfortless: I will come to you.'"*

The Sufficiency of His Words

Take whichever of the words you will, and they each sparkle and gleam in this manner. Observe, too, the richness and sufficiency of the text: *"I will not leave you comfortless: I will come to you."* He does not promise, "I will send you sanctifying grace, sustaining mercy, or precious mercy," but He says the only thing that will prevent you from being orphans: *"I will come to you."*

Ah, Lord! Your grace is sweet, but You are better. The vine is good, but the clusters are better. It is well enough to have a gift from Your hand, but oh, to touch the hand itself! It is well enough to hear the words of Your lips, but oh, to kiss those lips as the spouse did in the Song of Solomon! This is better still!

You know that you cannot prevent an orphan from remaining an orphan. You may feel great kindness toward the child, supply his needs, and do all you possibly can for him, but he is still an orphan. He must get his father and mother back, or else he will still be an orphan. Knowing this, our blessed Lord does not say, "I will do this and that for you," but, *"I will come to you."*

Do you not see, dear friends, here is not only all you can want, but also all you think you can want, wrapped up in a sentence, *"I will come to you"*? *"It pleased the Father that in him should all fulness dwell"* (Col. 1:19). Thus, when Christ comes, *"all fulness"* comes as well. *"In him dwelleth all the fulness of the Godhead bodily"* (Col. 2:9). Thus, when Jesus comes, the very Godhead comes to the believer. Observe, then, the language and the sufficiency of the promise.

A Continual Promise

I want you to notice, further, the continued freshness and force of the promise. If you owe someone fifty dollars and you give him a written promise to pay tomorrow, he will come to your house tomorrow and get the fifty dollars. What good is the written promise after that?

It has no further value; it is discharged. How would you like to have a written promise that would always stand good? That would be a great gift. "I promise to pay forever, and this bond, though paid a thousand times, will still hold good." Who would not like to have a check of that sort? Yet this is the promise that Christ gives you: *"I will not leave you orphans: I will come to you."*

The first time a sinner looks to Christ, Christ comes to him. And then what? Why, the next minute it is still, *"I will come to you."* But suppose someone has known Christ for fifty years, and he has had this promise fulfilled a thousand times a year. Is the promise done with then, after fifty thousand times? Certainly not! It stands just as fresh as when Jesus first spoke it: *"I will come to you."*

When we understand this, we will take our Lord at His word. We will go to Him as often as we can, for we will never weary Him. And when He has kept His promise most, then we will go to Him and ask Him to keep it more still. And after ten thousand proofs of the truth of it, we will only have a greater hungering and thirsting to get it fulfilled again. This is our blessed provision: *"I will come to you."* In the last moment, when your pulse beats faintly and you are just about to pass away and enter into the invisible world, you may have this upon your lips and say to your Lord, "My Master, still fulfill the word on which You have caused me to hope: *'I will not leave you comfortless: I will come to you.'"*

Entirely Valid

Let me remind you that the text is at this moment valid, and for this reason I delight in it. *"I will not leave you comfortless."* That means now, *"I will not leave you comfortless* [now]." Are you comfortless right now? It is your own fault. Jesus Christ does not leave you so, nor does He make you so. There are rich and precious things in this word: *"I will not leave you comfortless: I will come to you,"* that is, *"I will come to you* [now]."

You may be going through a very dry spiritual time, and you may be longing to come nearer to Christ. Then plead the promise before the Lord. Plead the promise as you sit where you are: "Lord, You have said You will come to me; come to me now." There are many reasons, believer, why you should plead in this way. You want Him, you need Him, you require Him; therefore, plead the promise and expect its fulfillment.

And oh, when He comes, what a joy it is! He is as a bridegroom coming out of his chamber with his garments fragrant with aloes and cassia (Ps. 45:8)! How the oil of joy will perfume your heart! How soon will your sackcloth be put away, and garments of gladness will adorn you! With great joy in your heart, your heavy soul will begin to sing when Jesus Christ whispers that you are His and that He is yours! Come, my Beloved, do not hesitate; *"be thou like a roe or a young hart upon the mountains of* [division]" (Song 2:17), and prove Your promise: *"I will not leave you orphans: I will come to you."*

Many Do Not Share in This Promise

And now, let me remind you that there are many who have no share in the promise of our text. What can I say to such people? I pity you who do not know what the love of Christ means. Oh, if you could only see the joy of God's people, you would not rest an hour without it.

His worth, if all the nations knew,
Sure the whole world would love Him too.

Remember, if you want to find Christ, He is to be found in the way of faith. Trust Him, and He is yours. Depend on the merit of His sacrifice; cast yourself entirely upon that, and you are saved, and Christ is yours.

Chapter 15

The Sin-Bearer

*Who his own self bare our sins in his own
body on the tree, that we, being dead to sins,
should live unto righteousness: by whose
stripes ye were healed. For ye were as
sheep going astray; but are now returned
unto the Shepherd and Bishop of your souls.
—1 Peter 2:24–25*

This wonderful passage is part of Peter's address to servants, and in his day nearly all servants were slaves. Peter began by saying,

¹⁸ *Servants, be subject to your masters with all fear; not only to the good and gentle, but also to the froward.*

¹⁹ *For this is thankworthy, if a man for conscience toward God endure grief, suffering wrongfully.*

²⁰ *For what glory is it, if, when ye be buffeted for your faults, ye shall take it patiently? but if, when ye do well, and suffer for it, ye take it patiently, this is acceptable with God.*

²¹ *For even hereunto were ye called: because Christ also suffered for us, leaving us an example, that ye should follow his steps:*

²² *who did no sin, neither was guile found in his mouth:*
²³ *who, when he was reviled, reviled not again; when he suffered, he threatened not; but committed himself to him that judgeth righteously:*
²⁴ *who his own self bare our sins in his own body on the tree, that we, being dead to sins, should live unto righteousness: by whose stripes ye were healed.*

(1 Pet. 2:18–24)

If we are in a humble condition of life, we will find our best comfort in thinking of the humble Savior bearing our sins in all patience and submission. If we are called to suffer, as servants often were in Roman times, we will be comforted by a vision of our Lord buffeted, scourged, and crucified, yet silent in the majesty of His endurance. If these sufferings are entirely undeserved and we are grossly slandered, we will be comforted by remembering Him who committed no sin and in whose lips no guile was found. Our Lord Jesus is Head of the Guild of Sufferers: He did good, and suffered for it, but He took it patiently. Our support in carrying our cross, which we are appointed to bear, is only to be found in Him *"who...bare our sins in his own body on the tree."*

We ourselves now know by experience that there is no place for comfort like the Cross. It is a tree stripped of all foliage, apparently dead; yet we sit under its shadow with great delight, and its fruit is sweet to our taste (Song 2:3). Truly, in this case, like cures like. By the suffering of our Lord Jesus, our suffering is made easy. The servant is comforted since Jesus took upon Himself the form of a servant; the sufferer is encouraged *"because Christ also suffered for us"* (1 Pet. 2:21); and the slandered one is strengthened because Jesus also was reviled.

As we hope to pass through the tribulations of this world, let us stand fast by the Cross; for if that is gone, the star is extinguished whose light cheers the down-trodden, shines on the injured, and brings light to the oppressed. If we lose the Cross, if we miss the substitutionary sacrifice of our Lord Jesus Christ, we have lost everything.

The verses that I quoted at the beginning of this chapter speak of three things: the bearing of our sins, the changing of our condition, and the healing of our spiritual diseases. Each of these deserves our most careful notice.

The Bearing of Our Sins

Literally

The first thing is the bearing of our sins by our Lord, *"who his own self bare our sins in his own body on the tree."* These words plainly assert that our Lord Jesus really did bear the sins of His people. How literal the language is! Words mean nothing if Christ's substitutionary sacrifice is not indicated here, and I do not know the meaning of Isaiah 53 if this is not its meaning. Read the prophet's words: *"The LORD hath laid on him the iniquity of us all"* (Isa. 53:6); *"for the transgression of my people was he stricken"* (v. 8); *"he shall bear their iniquities"* (v. 11); *"he was numbered with the transgressors; and he bare the sin of many"* (v. 12).

I cannot imagine that the Holy Spirit would have used language so expressive if He had not intended to teach us that our Savior really did bear our sins and suffer in our place. What else can be intended by texts like these: *"Christ was once offered to bear the sins of many"*

(Heb. 9:28); *"he hath made him to be sin for us, who knew no sin; that we might be made the righteousness of God in him"* (2 Cor. 5:21); *"Christ hath redeemed us from the curse of the law, being made a curse for us: for it is written, Cursed is every one that hangeth on a tree"* (Gal. 3:13); *"Christ also hath loved us, and hath given himself for us an offering and a sacrifice to God for a sweetsmelling savour"* (Eph. 5:2); *"once in the end of the world hath he appeared to put away sin by the sacrifice of himself"* (Heb. 9:26)? These Scriptures either teach the bearing of our sins by our Lord Jesus, or they teach nothing.

In these days, among many errors and denials of truth, there has sprung up a teaching of "modern thought" that explains away the doctrine of substitution and vicarious sacrifice. Some have gone so far as to say that the transference of sin or righteousness is impossible, and others of the same school have stigmatized the idea as immoral.

It does not much matter what these modern haters of the Cross may dare to say. Assuredly, that which they deny, denounce, and deride is the cardinal doctrine of our most holy faith and is as clearly in Scripture as the sun is in the heavens. Beloved, as we suffer through the sin of Adam, so are we saved through the righteousness of Christ. Our fall was caused by another, and so is our rising again. We are under a system of representation and imputation, no matter what anyone says against it. To us, the transference of our sin to Christ is a blessed fact clearly revealed in the Word of God and graciously confirmed in the experience of our faith.

In that same chapter of Isaiah we read, *"Surely he hath borne our griefs, and carried our sorrows"* (Isa. 53:4), and we perceive that this was a fact, for He was really, truly, and emphatically sorrowful. Therefore, when we read that He *"bare our sins in his own body on the tree,"* we dare not take it lightly. We believe that in very deed He was our Sin-Bearer. Possible or impossible, we sing with full assurance, "He bore on the tree the sentence for me."

If the sorrow had been figurative, the sin-bearing might have been a mere myth, but the one fact is paralleled by the other. There is no mere illustration in our text; it is a bare, literal fact: *"Who his own self bare our sins in his own body on the tree."* Oh, if only people would give up raising trivial objections to this! To question and debate the Cross is like the crime of the Roman soldiers when they divided His garments among themselves and cast lots for His clothing.

Personally

Next, note how personal are the terms used here! The Holy Spirit is very explicit: *"Who his own self bare our sins in his own body."* It was not by delegation, but *"his own self,"* and it was not in someone's imagination, but *"in his own body."* Observe, also, the personal aspect from our side of the question: He *"bare our sins"*—my sins and your sins. As surely as it was Christ's own self that suffered on the cross, so truly were they our own sins that Jesus bore *"in his own body on the tree."*

Our Lord has appeared in court for us, accepting our place at the stand: *"he was numbered with the transgressors"* (Isa. 53:12). Moreover, He has appeared at the place of execution for us and has borne the death penalty upon the gallows of doom in our place. *In propriâ personâ,* our Redeemer has been arraigned, though innocent; has come under the curse, though forever blessed;

and has suffered to the death, though He had done nothing worthy of blame. *"He was wounded for our transgressions, he was bruised for our iniquities: the chastisement of our peace was upon him; and with his stripes we are healed"* (Isa. 53:5).

Continually

The sin-bearing on our Lord's part is also continual. This passage in 1 Peter has been forced beyond its meaning; people have used it to assert that our Lord Jesus bore our sins nowhere but on the cross. But the words do not say this. *"The tree"* was the place where, beyond all other places, we see our Lord bearing the chastisement for our sins. But before this, He had felt the weight of the enormous load. It is wrong to base a great doctrine upon the incidental form of one passage of Scripture, especially when that passage of Scripture bears another meaning.

In the Revised Version, the marginal note for this passage reads, *"Who his own self carried up our sins in his body to the tree."* Our Lord carried the burden of our sins up to the tree, and there and then He made an end of it. He had carried that load long before, for John the Baptist said of Him, *"Behold the Lamb of God, which taketh away* [the verb is in the present tense] *the sin of the world"* (John 1:29). Our Lord was then bearing the sin of the world as the Lamb of God. From the day when He began His divine ministry, and even before that, He bore our sins.

He was the Lamb *"slain from the foundation of the world"* (Rev. 13:8); so, when He went up to Calvary, bearing His cross, He was bearing our sins up to the tree. Especially in the agony of His death, He stood in our place, and upon His soul and body burst the tempest of justice that had gathered through our transgressions.

Finally

This sin-bearing is final. He bore our sins *"in his own body on the tree,"* but now He bears them no longer. The sinner and the sinner's Surety are both free, for the law is vindicated, the substitutionary sacrifice is complete. He dies no more; death no longer has dominion over Him, for He has ended His work and has cried, *"It is finished"* (John 19:30). As for the sins that He bore in His own body on the tree, they cannot be found, for they have ceased to exist.

This is according to that ancient promise:

[20] *In those days, and in that time, saith the LORD, the iniquity of Israel shall be sought for, and there shall be none; and the sins of Judah, and they shall not be found.* (Jer. 50:20)

The work of the Messiah was *"to finish the transgression, and to make an end of sins, and to make reconciliation for iniquity, and to bring in everlasting righteousness"* (Dan. 9:24). Now, if sin is brought to an end, nothing more needs to be done; and if transgression is finished, there is no more to be said about it.

Effectively

Let us look back with holy faith and see Jesus bearing the stupendous load of our sins up to the tree and on the tree. His sacrifice discharged the whole mass of our moral liability both in reference to guiltiness in the sight of God and to the punishment that follows! It is a law of nature that nothing can be in two places at the same time, and if sin was borne away by our Lord, it cannot rest upon us. If by faith we have accepted the Substitute whom God Himself has accepted, then it is not possible for the penalty to be demanded twice, first of the Surety and then of those for whom He stood.

The Lord Jesus bore the sins of His people away, even as the scapegoat carried the sin of Israel to an uninhabited land. Our sins are gone forever. *"As far as the east is from the west, so far hath he removed our transgressions from us"* (Ps. 103:12). He has cast all our iniquities into the depths of the sea; He has hurled them behind His back, where they will be seen no more.

Beloved friends, we very calmly and coolly talk about this thing, but it is the greatest marvel in the universe. It is the miracle of earth, the mystery of heaven, the terror of hell. If we could fully realize the guilt of sin, the punishment due for it, and the literal substitution of Christ, it would give us an intense enthusiasm of gratitude, love, and praise. This is enough to make us all shout and sing, as long as we live, "Glory, glory to the Son of God!"

What an amazing thing that the Prince of Glory, in whom there is no sin, who was indeed incapable of evil, should condescend to come into such contact with our sin by being *"made...sin for us"* (2 Cor. 5:21)! Our Lord Jesus did not handle sin with golden tongs, but He bore it on His own shoulders. He did not lift it with golden staffs, as the priests carried the ark, but He Himself bore the hideous load of our sin *"in his own body on the tree."* This is the mystery of grace that angels desire to look into (1 Pet. 1:12).

The Sin-Bearer

THE CHANGE IN OUR CONDITION

In the second place, notice the change in our condition, which the text describes as the result of the Lord's bearing of our sins: *"That we, being dead to sins, should live unto righteousness."* The change is a dying and a reviving, a burial and a resurrection. We are brought from life to death and from death to life.

Dead to the Punishment for Sin

We are legally dead to the punishment for sin from this point onward. If I were condemned to die for an offense, and someone else died in my place, then I died in the one who died for me. The law could not lay the charge against me a second time, bring me before the judge again, condemn me, and lead me out to die. Where would be the justice of such a procedure? I am dead already; how can I die again?

Likewise, I have borne the wrath of God in the person of my glorious and ever blessed Substitute; how then can I bear it again? What was the use of a Substitute if I am to bear it also? If Satan were to come before God to lay an accusation against me, the answer would be, "This man is dead. He has borne the penalty, and is *'dead to sins,'* for the sentence against him has been executed upon Another." What a wonderful deliverance for us! Bless the Lord, O my soul!

Actually Dead to Sins

But Peter also meant to remind us that, through the influence of Christ's death upon our hearts, the Holy Spirit has made us now to be actually *"dead to sins."* In other words, we no longer love them, and they have ceased to hold dominion over us. Sin is no longer at home in our hearts; if it enters there, it is as an intruder. We are no longer its willing servants. Sin calls to us by temptation, but we give it no answer, for we are deaf to its voice. Sin promises us a high reward, but we do not consent, for we are dead to its allurements.

We sin, but our will is not to sin. It would be heaven to us to be perfectly holy. Our hearts and lives pursue perfection, but sin is abhorred by our souls. *"Now if I do that I would not, it is no more I that do it, but sin that dwelleth in me"* (Rom 7:20). Our truest and most real self hates sin, yet we fall into it. Even so, we run from the evil of sin with the greatest speed, for the new life within us has no dealings with sin; it is dead to sin.

The Greek word used here cannot be fully translated into English. It signifies "being unborn to sins." We were born in sin, but by the death of Christ and the work of the Holy Spirit in us, that birth is undone. We are actually "unborn" to sins. What was in us by sin, even at our birth, is through the death of Jesus counteracted by the new life that His Spirit imparts. We are unborn to sins. I like the phrase, as unusual as it may seem. Does it seem possible that birth can be reversed—that the born can be unborn? Yet it is so. The true ego, the "I," is now unborn to sins, for we are *"born, not of blood, nor of the will of the flesh, nor of the will of man, but of God"* (John 1:13). We are unborn to sins and born unto God.

Brought into Life

Our Lord's sin-bearing has also brought us into life. Dead to evil according to law, we also live in newness of life in the kingdom of grace. Our Lord's objective is *"that we...should live unto righteousness.*" Not only are our lives to be righteous, which I trust they are, but we are made alive and made sensitive and vigorous in righteousness. Through our Lord's death, our eyes, our thoughts, our lips, and our hearts are renewed unto righteousness. Certainly, if the doctrine of His atoning sacrifice does not bring life to us, nothing will. When we sin, it is the sorrowful result of our former death; but when we work righteousness, we throw our whole souls into it. *"We...live unto righteousness."*

Because our divine Lord has died, we feel that we must use ourselves for His praise. The tree that brought death to our Savior is a tree of life to us. Sit under this true Tree of Life, and you will shake off the weakness and disease that came in by that Tree of Knowledge of Good and Evil. David Livingstone, the Scottish missionary to Africa, used certain medicines that were known as Livingstone's Rousers. But the glorious truths that are extracted from the bitter wood of the cross are far better rousers! Dear readers, let us show in our lives what wonders our Lord Jesus has accomplished for us by His agony and bloody sweat, by His cross and passion!

THE HEALING OF OUR DISEASES

The apostle then wrote of the healing of our diseases by Christ's death: *"By whose stripes ye were healed. For ye were as sheep going astray; but are now returned unto the Shepherd and Bishop of your souls."* We were healed, and we remain so. It is not a thing to be accomplished in the future; it has been done already. Peter described our disease in verse twenty-five. What was the nature of our sickness, then?

We Were Like Animals

First, it was brutishness. *"Ye were as sheep."* Sin has made us so that we are only fit to be compared to beasts, and to those of the least intelligence. The Scripture compares the unregenerate man to *"a wild ass's colt"* (Job 11:12). Amos compared Israel to the *"kine* [cattle] *of Bashan"* (Amos 4:1), and he said to them, *"Ye shall go out at the breaches, every cow at that which is before her"* (v. 3). David compared himself to a huge animal: *"So foolish was I, and ignorant: I was as a beast before thee"* (Ps. 73:22). We are nothing better than beasts until Christ comes to us.

But we are not beasts after that! A living, heavenly, spiritual nature is created within us when we come into contact with our Redeemer. We still carry around with us the old brutish nature, but by the grace of God it is put in subjection and kept there. Our fellowship now is with the Father and with His Son Jesus Christ. We *"were as sheep,"* but we are now men redeemed unto God.

We Were Prone to Wander

We are cured also of our tendency to wander, which is so common in sheep. *"Ye were as sheep going astray"*— always going astray, loving to go astray, delighting in it, never so happy as when we were wandering away from the fold. We wander still, but not as sheep wander. We now seek the right way and desire to *"follow the Lamb whithersoever he goeth"* (Rev. 14:4). If we wander, it is through ignorance or temptation. We can truly say, *"My soul followeth hard after thee"* (Ps. 63:8). Our Lord's cross has securely nailed our hands and feet. Now we cannot run greedily after iniquity. Instead, we say, *"Return unto thy rest, O my soul; for the LORD hath dealt bountifully with thee"* (Ps. 116:7).

We Were Unable to Return

Another disease of ours was an inability to return: *"Ye were as sheep going astray; but are now returned."* Dogs, and even swine, are more likely to return home than wandering sheep. But now, beloved, though we wandered, we have returned and still do return to our Shepherd. Like Noah's dove, we have found no rest anywhere outside of the ark; and therefore we return to Him, and He graciously pulls us in to Himself. If we wander at any time, we bless God that there is something sacred within us that will not let us rest, and that there is a far more powerful Something above us that draws us back.

We are like the needle in a compass: touch the needle with your finger, force it to point to the east or to the south, and it may do so for a moment; but take away the pressure, and in an instant it returns to the pole. We must go back to Jesus in the same way; we must return to the Bishop of our souls. Our souls cry, *"Whom have I in heaven but thee? and there is none upon earth that I desire beside thee"* (Ps. 73:25). Thus, by the virtue of our Lord's death, an immortal love is created in us that leads us to seek His face and renew our fellowship with Him.

We Were Ready to Follow Others

Our Lord's death has also cured us of our readiness to follow other leaders. If one sheep goes through a gap in the hedge, the whole flock will follow. We have been accustomed to following ringleaders in sin or in error. We have been too ready to follow custom and to do what is considered proper, respectable, and usual. But now we are resolved to follow none but Jesus, according to His Word: *"My sheep hear my voice, and I know them, and they follow me"* (John 10:27); *"a stranger will they not follow, but will flee from him: for they know not the voice of strangers"* (v. 5).

Personally, I am resolved to follow no human leader. Faith in Jesus creates a sacred independence of mind. We have learned such an entire dependence upon our crucified Lord that we have none to spare for men.

We Were Exposed to Wolves

Finally, when we were wandering we were like sheep exposed to wolves, but we are delivered from this by being near the Shepherd. We were in danger of death, in danger from the Devil, in danger from a thousand temptations, which, like ravenous beasts, prowled around us. Having ended our wandering, we are now in a place of safety. When the lion roars, we are driven closer to the Shepherd, and we rejoice that His staff protects us. He says,

> [27] *My sheep hear my voice, and I know them, and they follow me:*
> [28] *and I give unto them eternal life; and they shall never perish, neither shall any man pluck them out of my hand.*   (John 10:27–28)

What a wonderful work of grace has been brought about in us! We owe all this not to the teaching of Christ, though that has helped us greatly; not to the example of

Christ, though that is inspiring us to diligently imitate Him; but to His stripes: *"By whose stripes ye were healed."*

Dear reader, we preach Christ crucified because we have been saved by Christ crucified. His death is the death of our sins. We can never give up the doctrine of Christ's substitutionary sacrifice, for it is the power by which we hope to be made holy. Not only are we washed from guilt in His blood, but by that blood we also overcome sin. As long as breath or pulse remains in us, we can never conceal the blessed truth that *"his own self bare our sins in his own body on the tree, that we, being dead to sins, should live unto righteousness."* May the Lord help us to know much more of this than I can write, for Jesus Christ's sake! Amen.